Trust and Trauma

This interdisciplinary text brings together perspectives from leading psychoanalysts and modern Jewish philosophers to offer a unique investigation into the dynamic between the fundamental trust in the self, other persons, and the world, and the devastating force of emotional trauma.

Chapters examine the challenges of witnessing and acknowledging suffering; trust in God; and the traumatic effects of the Holocaust. The result is a deeper understanding of the fundamental relationality of humans, the imperative of responsibility for the Other, the fragility of meaning, and the metaphorical powers of religious language. Authors representing two standpoints, the psychological/psychoanalytic and the religious/philosophical, provide key insights. Erik Erikson, Jessica Benjamin, Judith Herman, and Bessel van der Kolk support the psychological discourse, while Franz Rosenzweig, Martin Buber, and Abraham Joshua Heschel present the Jewish philosophical discourse.

This book is written for professionals and advanced students in psychoanalysis, philosophy, and Jewish and religious studies. Its accessible and engaging style will also appeal to general readers with an interest in philosophical, psychological, and religious perspectives on some of the most elemental human concerns.

Michael Oppenheim is a distinguished professor emeritus at Concordia University, Montreal. His most recent book is *Contemporary Psychoanalysis and Modern Jewish Philosophy: Two Languages of Love* (Routledge, 2017).

"Trust, so precious yet so fragile, forms for Oppenheim the crux of what psychological trauma shatters, in unexpected losses, torture, relentless humiliation, and the rest. This book will become indispensable reading for clinicians working to restore some fraction of the stability that trust in self, others, and world can provide. This work is thorough and nuanced, but still extremely readable."

Donna M. Orange, New York University Postdoctoral
Program in Psychoanalysis and Psychotherapy

"Frequently placed under the jurisdiction of psychology and neuroscience, the terms 'trauma' and 'trust' are often considered through secular frames, forgetting the rich insights and conversations within religious traditions. Oppenheim, as in his previous works, provides a gentle yet provocative call to hold discourses side-by-side and have them speak. This book allows these voices to complement one another and elevates questions that are core to human experience and struggle. Few scholars achieve what Oppenheim does in *Trust and Trauma* and this is a welcome addition to the interdisciplinary literature."

David M. Goodman, associate dean; and associate professor,
Counseling, Developmental, and Educational Psychology,
Boston College

"Once again, Michael Oppenheim has embarked upon uncharted territory, this time by researching and exploring relationships between two ostensibly disparate and opposing areas of human experience: trust and trauma. Through adventurous study of and engagement with the writings of key contemporary psychoanalysts and modern Jewish philosophers, Oppenheim unfolds his own unique insights and thereby evokes reflections on what, to varying degrees, we have all experienced and encountered. His clear albeit passionate style inspires in readers the courage to better and more deeply face those perennial challenges in our common quest for human meaning."

Barbara E. Galli, former Judaic Studies chair,
University of Alabama

The Psychology and the Other Book Series
Series Editor: David M. Goodman

Associate Editors: Brian W. Becker, Donna M. Orange, Eric R. Severson

The *Psychology and the Other* Book Series highlights creative work at the intersections between psychology and the vast array of disciplines relevant to the human psyche. The interdisciplinary focus of this series brings psychology into conversation with continental philosophy, psychoanalysis, religious studies, anthropology, sociology, and social/critical theory. The cross-fertilization of theory and practice, encompassing such a range of perspectives, encourages the exploration of alternative paradigms and newly articulated vocabularies that speak to human identity, freedom, and suffering. Thus, we are encouraged to reimagine our encounters with difference, our notions of the "other," and what constitutes therapeutic modalities.

The study and practices of mental health practitioners, psychoanalysts, and scholars in the humanities will be sharpened, enhanced, and illuminated by these vibrant conversations, representing pluralistic methods of inquiry, including those typically identified as psychoanalytic, humanistic, qualitative, phenomenological, or existential.

Series Titles:

Dante and the Other
A Phenomenology of Love
Aaron B. Daniels

Beyond Clinical Dehumanisation toward the Other in Community Mental Health Care
Levinas, Wonder and Autoethnography
Catherine A. Racine

Trust and Trauma
An Interdisciplinary Study in Human Nature
Michael Oppenheim

For a full list of titles in the series, please visit the Routledge website at: www.routledge.com/Psychology-and-the-Other/book-series/PSYOTH

Trust and Trauma

An Interdisciplinary Study
in Human Nature

Michael Oppenheim

Routledge
Taylor & Francis Group

LONDON AND NEW YORK

First published 2021
by Routledge
2 Park Square, Milton Park, Abingdon, Oxon OX14 4RN

and by Routledge
605 Third Avenue, New York, NY 10158

Routledge is an imprint of the Taylor & Francis Group, an informa business

British Library Cataloguing-in-Publication Data
A catalogue record for this book is available from the British Library

Library of Congress Cataloging-in-Publication Data
A catalog record for this title has been requested

ISBN: 978-0-367-45871-3 (hbk)
ISBN: 978-0-367-45870-6 (pbk)
ISBN: 978-1-003-02631-0 (ebk)

Typeset in Times New Roman
by Newgen Publishing UK

Noa and Maya,
to a new generation inspiring trust and hope in all of us

Contents

Author biography

Michael Oppenheim is a distinguished professor emeritus in the Department of Religions and Cultures of Concordia University, Montreal. His prior teaching and current research encompass modern Jewish philosophy, Jewish Studies, post-Freudian psychoanalysis, psychology of religion, and philosophy of religion. His books include: *Speaking/Writing of God: Jewish Philosophical Reflections on the Life with Others* (1997), *Jewish Philosophy and Psychoanalysis: Narrating the Interhuman* (2006), *Encounters of Consequence: Jewish Philosophy in the Twentieth Century and Beyond* (2009), and *Contemporary Psychoanalysis and Modern Jewish Philosophy: Two Languages of Love* (2017).

Preface

This interdisciplinary study of trust and trauma continues and extends many of the thematic and comparative interests exhibited in my earlier works. I have briefly written about what I now see as that fundamental trust, which provides the foundation for the self, as well as the relationships to others, and the world. In becoming increasingly aware of the profound multidisciplinary attention given to trauma, I began to see this psychological phenomenon as the mirror image of trust, and consequently realized that the exploration of each would provide an important portal into the other. This book also continues my focus on intersubjectivity. It is the importance of the life with others that long ago compelled my fascination with modern Jewish philosophers of encounter—particularly, Franz Rosenzweig, Martin Buber, and Emmanuel Levinas—and later with central figures in relational psychoanalysis—including Stephen Mitchell, Lewis Aron, and Jessica Benjamin. Intersubjectivity is also the single key to both trust and trauma. Trust's origin and its three-pronged reach over self, others and the world is mirrored by trauma's origin and the targets it devastates. Trust originates within the mother–infant dyad, while trauma only crystalizes in the absence of relational support.

The specific interdisciplinary dimension of this study illuminates the correlation between basic trust and trust in God. It allows the exploration of parallels between the psychological struggle with trauma's symptoms and the Jewish philosophical wrestling with some of the ramifications of the Holocaust. Together these examinations suggest that trust in God is not just some inscrutable, inconsequential feature of religious consciousness. It functions in many ways similar to basic trust, and can be equally as vulnerable or resilient to trauma.

Throughout my academic career I have been helped and supported by colleagues and students in the Department of Religions and Cultures at Concordia University, Montreal. I am particularly appreciative for this book to the careful reading and suggestions of the Psychology and the Other Book Series editor, David Goodman, and other members of the board. Barbara Galli has again been my first reader, whose enthusiasm has kept me going even when progress seemed elusive. As for over a decade, the insightful suggestions of my critic, personal editor, and loving son, David, have enriched the text in innumerable ways. Finally, I do sympathize with my wife, Sarah, for the difficulty of living with an obsessive, but loving, author. A version of Chapter 3 has appeared previously: Michael Oppenheim, "Not 'Any Tom, Dick, and Harry': Abraham Heschel and Martin Buber on the Holocaust," *Studies in Religion / Sciences Religieuses*, 44/3, pp. 334–355. Copyright c 2015 Sage Publishing. DOI: 10.1177/0008429815595809.

Introduction

"Turn it and turn it, for all is in it"[1]

The subject of trust and trauma reaches into a surfeit of topics, discourses, and genres, both historical and current. Preeminently, it is a portal into the very foundation of subjectivity. This is captured in Erik Erikson's eight-stage psychosocial diagram of development in which the first phase is appropriately titled "basic trust." He sees this quality as "the most fundamental prerequisite of mental vitality" (1968, 96), its absence signaling that life itself cannot go on. Emotional trauma stands at the opposite pole of trust, stopping everyday life in its tracks and eviscerating those elemental virtues that are featured in trust, particularly hope. In this light, the study of trust and trauma may be seen as a midrash on Sigmund Freud's all-encompassing dialectic of *eros* (the life instinct to connect and build up) and *thanatos* (the death instinct to tear down, approaching nothingness).

The inquiry into trust and trauma underscores the intricate psychological ties between the individual and others, a connection memorialized in Stephen Mitchell's words that "an individual human mind is an oxymoron; subjectivity always develops in the context of intersubjectivity" (2000, 57). This connection to others is especially germane here, exemplified in the emergence of trust in the mother–infant dyad, the radical alienation from others produced by trauma, and the crucial role of the support of therapists, friends, and fellow sufferers in recovery. More widely, throughout the stages of life there continues significant interaction by the child, adolescent, young adult, mature person, or the aged with a widening circle of others, from primary caregivers to the world at large. Possibly standing at the apex of intersubjectivity is what Erikson describes as mutual activation:

> *Mutual activation* is the crux of the matter ... [ego strength] depends from stage to stage upon a network of mutual influences within which the person actuates others even as he is actuated, and within which the person is "inspired with active properties," even as he so inspires others.
>
> (1964, 165)

There are both individual and communal dimensions to this exploration of trust and trauma. While the earliest months and years of infancy and childhood promise the first fruits of an ever-evolving trust, in extreme cases, through either neglect or abuse, they can be the site of debilitating developmental trauma. In later years women of all ages and young men, as well as religious and cultural minorities, are specifically vulnerable to traumatic episodes. The Holocaust and the atomic bombings of Hiroshima and Nagasaki have been primary foci for studies of the effects of collective trauma and the efforts at repair. Both trust, in the sense of a safe and lawful world, and trauma, in terms of chaos, violence, and calamity, are given communal and cultural expressions through myths, symbols, and historical narratives.

Explorations of individual and collective trauma have been pursued through a large variety of perspectives: psychological, philosophical, sociological, historical, religious, and literary. Although recent scholarship has offered significant critiques of the Western bias of many of these studies and the limits of their findings,[2] the events grouped together through the term "the Holocaust" offer a good example of this array of genres. Particularly noteworthy are the compelling literary efforts, ranging from famous non-fiction testimonials in diaries and memoirs—*The Diary of Anne Frank* or Primo Levi's *The Drowned and the Saved*—to powerful semi-fictional stories and novels—Elie Wiesel's *Night*.

Players and perspectives

Selected authors representing two of these perspectives, the psychological and the religious, will provide the key ingredients for this interdisciplinary examination. Erik Erikson's (1902–1994) description of the first stage of his psychosocial diagram of development, basic trust, supplies the primary material for understanding the nature and significance of this crucial mental quality. While the influence of this ego psychoanalyst has waned in many psychoanalytic circles since his death, the psychosocial arrangement with its elucidation of basic trust has retained its eminence in related fields, such as childhood development, early education, and adolescent studies (Schlein 2016, 19–20). Erikson elegantly portrays trust's singular importance at the beginning of life and its continual testing and evolution throughout later life crises. A number of features of his work are particularly germane to this study. The descriptions of all of the stages demonstrate how indispensable to the story of an individual's life is that widening circle of interaction with others. In a unique way Erikson blends the psychological purview with deep moral and even artistic concerns, what perhaps is meant by the intriguing statement by Yankelovich and Barrett, "His writings are 'so appealing because he smuggles the concept of the human spirit through the back door of psychoanalytic theory'" (quoted in Schlein 2016, 6). Additionally, related to the prior sentiments, Erikson has a profound appreciation for the personal and communal resources within the phenomenon of religion that afford support and direction throughout the struggles that punctuate one individual's life cycle.

The psychoanalyst Jessica Benjamin has been a leading theorist since the publication of her trilogy of works in the last quarter of the twentieth century that brought together feminist and relational streams. Her writings highlight the intricate generative dynamics of the mother–infant dyad, the importance of mutual recognition throughout early development, and an acute critique of misogynist cultural forces in the West. Particularly since the turn of the last century, she has worked with and written about the victims of both individual and collective trauma. This includes her patients suffering from developmental trauma and episodes of violence, as well as those impacted by Apartheid in South Africa and the Israeli–Palestinian conflict. Themes that emerge from this later work include the obligation to witness and acknowledge injury and injustice, and the importance of an underlying trust in a wider moral order for those struggling to recover.

Two of the leading contemporary psychiatrists in the field of trauma are introduced here to present a multifaceted phenomenology of the pathology and the tested paths for recovery. Judith Herman's work demonstrates the pertinence of gender in investigating the historical and ongoing locus of trauma's violence. In *Trauma and Recovery* (first published in 1992 with the latest edition in 2015) she combines this feminist conviction with an appreciation for other classes of vulnerable persons, especially children, adolescent women, and young men at war, writing, "Rape and combat might thus be considered complementary social rites of initiation into the coercive violence at the foundations of adult society" (2015, 61). Her detailed, systematic presentation of traumatic disorders along with a three-stage prescription for recovery—Safety, Remembrance and Mourning, Reconnection—have been taken as milestones in trauma treatment. In addition, and especially relevant to the present investigation, Herman at times utilizes Erikson's diagram of psychosocial stages and his analysis of basic trust in understanding the psychological bases of health and the functions that trauma targets.

Bessel van der Kolk's *The Body Keeps the Score* (2015) is the culmination of decades of research and therapeutic encounters. He brings together a thorough phenomenology of trauma syndromes with thoughtful assessments of current programs of repair. Particularly of note is his deep appreciation for the role of supportive relations with others and his sensitive approach to the intractable and disheartening area of childhood trauma.

The major resources for exploring the nature of religious trust are two of the most significant, and contemporarily relevant, modern Jewish philosophers, Martin Buber (1878–1965) and Franz Rosenzweig (1886–1929). Buber's understanding of the Hebrew term *emunah* (faith) in terms of trust[3] sets the stage for this approach. For Buber, this fundamental trust encompasses the individual's "whole life, that is in the actual totality of his relationships, not only towards God, but also to his appointed sphere in the world and to himself" (2003b, 40). The objects of this passion are thus: oneself, other persons, the world, and God. Buber's book *I and Thou*[4] is a template for how the dialogic encounter with others and with God leads to the living out of this four-fold trust.

In two of his later essays, as well as his *The Star of Redemption*, Rosenzweig explores the nature as well as the parameters of religious trust or trust in God. He is particularly interested in trust in language or speech, that is to say, a trust that the deepest experiences in human life can be communicated and shared with others. Beyond this, he sees the relationship to God involving trust in experience, the meaningfulness of life, one's community, and in humans themselves. Further, Rosenzweig examines how trust provides the foundation for other essential human qualities. He writes, "To walk humbly with your God—nothing more is asked for here than a wholly present trust," which is the "seed from which faith, hope and love grow, and the fruit that ripens from it" (2005, 447).

Although they escaped the direct violence of the Holocaust, Abraham Joshua Heschel (1907–1972) and Buber undertook serious philosophic confrontations with what the former spoke of as the experience of being "a brand plucked from the fire, in which my people was burned to death" (Heschel 2009, 3). While the majority of their post-Holocaust writings celebrate a vibrant trust in God, elements of doubt and anguish repeatedly intercede. Heschel marshals a litany of traditional Jewish responses to horror and suffering—it is the fault of humans and not God; this is the negative side of the gift of human freedom; a heavenly reward awaits the righteous; what right do humans have to question the creator of it all?—but at the end he also allows for "the thought that ultimately God Himself was responsible for the inherent falsehood of human existence" (1974, 233). The markedly untraditional Buber is left weighing metaphors of a divine eclipse, and God's silence, yet still voicing a halting trust: "I know what it means to cling to Him" (2003a, 173). In all, their struggles are important resources for understanding religious trust on trial.

There are other voices introduced into this study, those of both psychologists and philosophers. Among those are persons who represent what Donna Orange described as one's "internal chorus" (2016, xi). These are persons whose work has become so much a part of me that I constantly, seemingly unintentionally, evoke their ideas and concerns whenever I think or read about pertinent existential issues. The words of the Jewish philosopher Emmanuel Levinas (1906–1995) directly appear throughout this text in conjunction with his response to the Holocaust and, expressly, his philosophy of the ineluctable responsibility for the other. There are rare references to the Danish Christian philosopher Søren Kierkegaard (1813–1855), but he is latent everywhere. Borrowing Levinas' sentiment about Rosensweig's *Star* in conjunction with his own major work, *Totality and Infinity*, the Danish existentialist is almost "too often present in this book to be cited" (1969, 28). As will be apparent below, the approach of the philosopher and psychologist William James (1842–1910), specifically as manifest in his classic *The Varieties of Religious Experience*, has an important presence. Some of the other members of this chorus have already been presented: Rosenzweig, Buber, Erikson, and Stephen Mitchell, who makes a number of appearances in the text. Together they help to make my engagement with basic trust and its enigmatic rupture almost inevitable.

A few important methodological insights have influenced the approach of this study into trust and trauma. Through a single sentence in the *Varieties*, James justifies his commitment to a plurality of avenues to truth, writing, "And why, after all, may not the world be so complex as to consist of many interpenetrating spheres of reality, which we can thus approach in alternation by using different conceptions and assuming different attitudes" (2004, 92). This sentiment is one aspect behind the use of the Talmudic expression—"Turn it and turn it, for all is in it"—that serves as the epigram for this Introduction.

Richard Rorty's (1931–2007) much cited essay "Pragmatism and Philosophy" describes a shift in how Western philosophy itself is seen. He distinguishes between "Philosophy" and "philosophy." Thinkers who believe in "Philosophy" search for ultimate truths that transcend cultures, languages, and particular discourses. Adherents of "philosophy" "compare and contrast cultural traditions" and find that "in the process of playing vocabularies and cultures off against each other, we produce new and better ways of talking and acting" (1987, 54). These post-philosophical philosophers study "the comparative advantages and disadvantages of the various ways of talking that our race has invented" (58).

Lastly, in "The New Thinking" of 1925 Rosenzweig describes a principle that releases the full potential of an engagement between religious discourse and the challenges of everyday life. He writes, "Theological problems are to be translated into the human, and the human driven forward until they reach the theological" (1999a, 89). Rosenzweig adds that by the "theological" he does not mean "theological thinking" (88), which is why the label of "religious discourse" seems an appropriate conversion.

These three brief guidelines can be seen to expeditiously blend together. In exploring our "complex" world, and in particular its human expanse, multiple cultural, disciplinary, and discursive approaches are required. The specific multidisciplinary presentation utilized here, rather than being seen as somehow exhaustive, should be taken as an invitation to even further cultural and disciplinary contributions. Accompanying this affirmation of the ultimate value of pluralistic avenues is the persistent rejection of all reductionist tendencies.

The goal of this study is to widen and deepen the ways we understand and address key features of our lives. Particular discourses must be tested, through dialogue, as it were, to reveal their strengths and weaknesses, powers and limits, and in the end to identify areas of possible cross-fertilization. The concentration on producing "new and better ways of talking and acting" necessarily eschews statements about ultimate truth or metaphysical claims.

"Theological" or religious discourses are valued in this perspective for offering powerful insights into the nature and meaning of human existence. They broaden and deepen our purview through their language about a transcendent dimension in our lives, opening up possibilities for radical transformation, that is, surprise.[5] While every discourse utilizes a specific cast of metaphors at its core, the necessarily metaphoric, even poetic style of religious discourse issues from its exhortation to the transcendent.

The five chapters and conclusion that follow can be seen to comprise three sections. The psychological perspective on trust and trauma begins with a case study by Benjamin (Chapter 1) of collective and individual trauma. This is followed (Chapter 2) by a more systematic treatment, focusing particularly on the work of Erikson, Herman, and Van der Kolk. The section devoted to the Jewish philosophical purview is introduced (Chapter 3) through a case study of Heschel's and Buber's confrontation with the Holocaust. This leads (Chapter 4) to a more ordered examination of trust and trauma in the work of Rosenzweig, Buber, Heschel, and a few others. The last part is explicitly comparative: first (Chapter 5) juxtaposing the psychological and Jewish philosophical approaches, and finishing (Conclusion) with a retrospective employing points of departure by the psychologists James, Mitchell, and D. W. Winnicott.

Notes

1 Rabbi Ben Bag Bag, *Pirke Avot* 5:25 (Berkson and Fisch 2010, 180). I have borrowed what the rabbis saw as a statement about the grandeur of the Torah, to refer to the breadth of the dialectic of trust and trauma.
2 In the Preface to the edited volume *The Future of Trauma Theory: Contemporary Literary and Cultural Criticism*, Michael Rothberg writes, "We cannot assume that a category crafted in Europe and North America can travel smoothly to all other cultural locations: 'the PTSD construct reflects a Eurocentric, monocultural orientation.'" (Buelens, Durrant, and Eaglestone 2014, xii).
3 In *Two Types of Faith*, Buber finds that this trust in the Jewish case is focused on a person, rather than in early Christianity, where it designates the trust in some truth. However, he also makes the point that the Jewish sense of *emunah* is later found again and again in Christianity (2003b, 11–12).
4 While Walter Kaufmann translates Buber's book title *Ich und Du* as *I and Thou*, he translates the German *Du* as "You" throughout the text of his translation. He explains this decision in his "Prologue" to Buber's text (Buber 1970, 14–15). However, I continue to use "Thou" rather than "You" when quoting from his translation.
5 Buber's notion of "fettered surprise" is discussed in the author's *Jewish Philosophy and Psychoanalysis* (Oppenheim 2006, 171). For Buber, while an individual's past has some influence on their character and actions, there is also an incalculable feature to the human spirit that leaves the present and future open-ended. This is similar to what Kierkegaard meant in the pseudonymous *The Sickness unto Death* by the self's dialectic between necessity and possibility or finitude and infinitude (1980, 29–42).

1 "The Moral Third"

Jessica Benjamin's examination of collective and individual trauma

Jessica Benjamin is one of the foremost thinkers and clinicians in the dynamic post-Freudian stream of Relational Psychoanalysis. In the last two decades of the twentieth century her writings focused on how recognition of the other as an independent subject plays a key, transformative role in individual development and flourishing. Increasingly, since the turn of the century, she addresses the plight of those who suffer from both collective and individual trauma. Particularly in terms of the former, she writes, "This represents an effort to show the possibilities for applying psychoanalytically derived concepts to social phenomena, and suggest ways in which recognition theory can be used to grasp deep psychological structures within both collective and individual processes" (2014a).

This study begins with an examination of some of the underlying features of Benjamin's recognition theory. This is followed by a presentation of her dynamic approach to collective trauma, in terms of the relationships between bystanders, victims, and perpetrators. The chapter continues with her clinical efforts to address patients who suffer from individual trauma. At the conclusion there is a discussion of her transformed vision of psychoanalysis that features the concept of the "moral third."

Intersubjectivity and recognition

Benjamin describes intersubjectivity, a crucial feature of her work, in terms of the relationship between one subject and an independent and outside other. In her words, "The problem of how we relate to the fact of the other's independent consciousness, a mind that is fundamentally like our own but unfathomably different and outside our control, has been a through line in my work" (1998, xii). It is in relationship with this outside other that humans initially develop and ultimately become full persons.

However, the path to this fullness is neither simple nor smooth. Humans are riddled by two conflicting desires. In Benjamin's words, "Our psychic makeup is such that we are torn between omnipotence, illusion of control, on the one hand, and the wish for contact with the different, the external, the not-me, on the other" (1999, 202). Omnipotence points to the process where the ego seeks to master what is different, that is, outside of itself. The other is either fantasized as being totally subservient to the self's desire or treated as a dangerous alien figure that must be destroyed. Further, since the other person is subject to the same inner psychological processes, in every relationship there is an inevitable conflict of wills. There is a tension between a resolution in either domination of or submission to the other, and in this regard, Benjamin often turns to Hegel's portrayal of the master/slave dynamic (1988, 32–33).

The second desire is toward making contact with what is outside and different—with another mind. It is in this regard that Benjamin's concept of recognition is featured. Humans are fundamentally social creatures. They find pleasure in being with others, in being appreciated by another for their uniqueness, and also in being excited by the other person who is different than themselves. In Benjamin's words, "We have a need for recognition and … we have a capacity to recognize others in return, thus making mutual recognition possible" (1995, 30).

The psychic tension between this fear of and longing for the other is never finally resolved. However, the basis for recognition is established because the other person can come to be experienced as someone similar to, rather than as totally different from the self. Experiences of identification—"by taking something in from the object, by assimilating the other to the self" (1988, 42–43)—and sharing feelings, which first occur between mother and child in infancy, are the foundation for accepting or recognizing the other. For example, sometimes this is formulated by Benjamin in terms of the alignment or attunement of feelings and actions between mother and infant: "For the sense of difference to be exciting and pleasurable rather than merely threatening, the self must be able to bear an attunement with the other that revives earlier feelings of identification" (1998, 70).

Benjamin's work reveals some startling insights arising from her attention to intersubjectivity. Two of these ideas concern the relational drama of "doer/done to," and the space beyond this struggle, demarcated as "the third." Doer and done to represents a complementary relation in which both sides feel that they are being dominated and manipulated by the other. Each person experiences a sense of helplessness, of being a victim, within a dynamic where it seems that the only escape is to take the upper hand. In this connection she explains, "It is as if the essence of complementary relations—the relation of twoness—is that there appear to be only two choices: either submission or resistance to the other's demand" (2012, 95).

For Benjamin, the concepts of the third and "thirdness" refer to an interactive space beyond the complementary relations of doer/done to and power/powerlessness. In a relation in which the third is appreciated there is an openness to the other, a respect for difference, and a shared experiencing of recognition.[1] She writes, "The third appears only in the relationship of recognition, the space that mediates the two partners' viewpoints,

preventing the collapse of tension" into the fruitless battle of complementarity (1999, 204). Lastly, one feature of the third she describes as
the "moral third." This involves the idea that in thirdness there is a moral
dimension, a respect for some "lawfulness," for "human dignity," and for
the value of human life overall that guides the relationship (2009, 447;
2012, 98; 2018, 51).

Benjamin has always demonstrated a commitment to understanding
what implications her psychoanalytic insights might have in combatting
social injustice and violence. This is well illustrated in her first book, *The
Bonds of Love* of 1988, where she explores the pernicious quality of gender
polarity, particularly the complementarity of (male) domination and
(female) submission, which pervades Western cultural and political life
(1988, 71–76). Her later reflection on the message of that text emphasized
the need and possibility of breaking out of the dialectic of power/power-
lessness. She writes, "I looked to a way to deconstruct rather than reverse
the binary of doer and done to and conceptualize a position in which
victims of oppression can demand liberation and empowerment without
retaliatory reversal of power relations" (2014a).

"Victim–Perpetrator–Bystander Relations"[2]

Benjamin offers a rich and intricate description of the primary actors and
dynamics, what she designates as "victim-perpetrator-bystander relations"
(2014a), which constitute the challenging arena of social violence, injury,
and trauma. While the three positions are obviously relational and essentially interwoven, to facilitate understanding they will be treated separately
below. Each will be presented in terms of the failure or success of recognition, that is to say: (1) what prevents recognition, and the consequences;
(2) how recognition is accomplished, and the results.

Bystanders

One of the main foci of Benjamin's latest work is the position of those individuals who stand outside the specific terrain demarcated by the concrete
acts of violence and the suffering of the victims. The significance of this
site is well illustrated in her most detailed treatment, "The Discarded and
the Dignified." The essay begins with an epigraph by the Holocaust survivor Primo Levi (1919–1987). In *The Drowned and the Saved*, Levi details
a haunting dream of many survivors, in which their traumatic experience is
left unacknowledged by the outside world:

> Strangely enough, this same thought ("even if we were to tell it,
> we would not be believed") arose in the form of nocturnal dreams
> produced by the prisoners' despair. Almost all the survivors, orally or
> in their written memoirs, remember a dream which frequently recurred
> during the nights of imprisonment, varied in its detail but uniform in

its substance: they had returned home and with passion and relief were describing their past sufferings, addressing themselves to a loved one, and were not believed, indeed were not even listened to. In the most typical (and cruelest) form, the interlocutor turned and left in silence.
                    (quoted in Benjamin 2014a; see also Benjamin 2018, 215)

Benjamin is particularly interested in what prevents the witness's acknowledgement of the victim's injury and trauma. In this connection she speaks of the passive bystander or "failed witness," writing, "This idea refers to a failure of those not involved in the acts of injury to serve the function of acknowledging and actively countering or repairing the suffering and injury that they encounter as observers in the social world" (2014a; 2018, 216). The bystander lacks identification and empathy with the victim. There is a dissociation from the concrete pain and suffering of the other. For Benjamin there are complicated, albeit resounding psychological dynamics behind the more general "faint-heartedness," self-protectiveness, fear, and guilt that hinder or even paralyze recognition (2014b).

The bystander is closed off from being empathetic with the victim's suffering; "a dissociation of the others' humanity" (Benjamin 2018, 231). That victim is felt to be unlike the self—or, actually, not even a full self or person. The condition of seeing the other as totally different is also the result of projective identification, in which rejected elements of the self—such as weakness and vulnerability—are projected onto the other (225–226). There is a psychological splitting between the dishonorable, failed, and guilty, and the worthy, successful, and righteous—ultimately between "the discarded" and "the dignified" (2014b; 2018, 226). Thus, the unacknowledged victims of violence are seen as both deserving of their plight and not to be grieved.

This splitting serves a number of purposes. It dissociates or disconnects the bystander from the suffering ones "in order to stave off the terror of sharing their fate" (Benjamin 2014b). Here the vulnerability of the self, the possible fate of oneself being abandoned and unrecognized, is buried beneath the illusion of being "invulnerable" and "triumphant" (2014a). This scenario is built upon what Benjamin features as the "complementarity position" that there are those "who may live and those who must die" (2014b). In the situation where "only one can live" (2014b; 2018, 229–230), the reality that all persons are vulnerable and the moral ideal that all deserve to live are spurned.

Another self-protective process behind the failed witness relates to the bystander's relation to the perpetrators of violence. There may be an identification with the aggressor, which again staves off the anxiety of oneself possibly being a victim. In turn the bystander may come to feel guilty about this form of identification and through a "manic defense" (Benjamin 2014b; 2018, 224) insist that the aggressor stands as an embodiment of pure evil, while the self is totally excluded from the monstrousness of the crimes. Benjamin explains,

Bystander guilt is not the guilt that can recognize the "badness" within the self, or acknowledge the commonality of destructive fantasies (fantasies of vengeance, of sibling triumph, from throwing the favored brother into a pit to holding a knife at the enemy's throat) but rather projectively offloads it onto the other.

(2014d)

There are, of course, communal dimensions to these psychological processes. Benjamin's research, especially in the context of the Israeli–Palestinian conflict, reveals how communal narratives and group identities act as a "barrier" to empathy for the suffering other and to acknowledging one's own community's responsibility for the injuries inflicted (2014c). Here she again sees a complementarity, in this case in the form of a "battle for recognition" (2014c), where only one side can be recognized and the other discarded. Members of communities who are in the midst of this form of social violence are also fully aware that speaking out for the suffering of the other side will inevitably ostracize them from family, friends, and the wider group: there is "us" and "them," but no viable, conscientious third position. In addition to the helplessness and paralyzing effect that these individual and group processes have in blocking identification with violence's specific victims, Benjamin is acutely concerned with the way that our feelings and connections to our fellow human beings, the community of all persons, are sundered.

Witnesses

The position of the witness, of what might be termed authentic witnessing, is essentially an active stance and the keystone of the edifice of repair. In this connection Benjamin frequently refers to South Africa's "Truth and Reconciliation Commission" (TRC) of 1996–1998 and to her own experience with the joint Israeli–Palestinian "Acknowledgement Project" (2018, 236–239), a series of dialogues between mental health practitioners of roughly 2004–2010. Her writings draw upon both of these intense exchanges, particularly in the case of the importance of public witnessing in affording dignity to the victim and in repairing social life.

Acknowledgement is a primary element in witnessing. Benjamin defines this as "dignifying and validating with our attention" (2014a). The dehumanization of the victim occurs through the double events of the initial violence and the lack of outside concern and response. In acknowledgement this is redressed through individual and public confirmation of the reality of the victim's suffering and the basic humanity or personhood of the injured.

If "dissociation" is one of the basic psychological processes behind the failed witness, identification and "embodiment" are the contrasting features of authentic witnessing. Whereas dissociation is a distancing and deadening of passion, embodiment, although difficult and painful, enlivens. The term accentuates the sense that the witness allows themself to empathize with the suffering to the extent of feeling as their own the injury to the concrete body of the victim. Thus, for Benjamin, embodiment is based upon the psychological process of identification, identifying with the suffering of the other. She speaks of "primal witnessing" and "primal identification" as "rooted in the primary embodied relations of recognition and attachment" (2014a; see also 2018, 224). Such primal witnessing also blocks the identification with the aggressor and its reversal in moralism.

Acknowledgement of the injury and trauma, identification with the suffering other, and recognition of the basic humanity of the victim undercut the splitting and complementarity that are featured in the bystander position. In identifying with and dignifying the victim, the witness no longer separates "us" from "them," "doer" from "done to," the safe, successful, and chosen from the exposed. Such splitting can only be overcome as the witness accepts the multiple dualities that abide within the self. Every human has the potential for being a victim or a perpetrator of violence. To illustrate this understanding, Benjamin refers to a Palestinian participant in the Acknowledgement Project:

> His action came from a deep understanding that accepting both perpetrator and victim sides of self, goodness and badness, breaks down the fictitious line between those who deserve mercy and hence to live, and those who do not; those who consign others to die and those who perish.
>
> (2014d; see also 2018, 245)

Benjamin often discusses this acceptance of the multiple sides of the self, particularly those that the individual would like to deny, in terms of the "monstrous," writing, "However, we all have a monstrous side, a side that wants to escape and deny pain, as well as a side that identifies with inflicting pain and transgression" (2014d; see also 2018, 243–244). The authentic witness must accept such badness within the self in order to be able to identify with the abject,[3] that is, the suffering victim, and to recognize the unconscious pull of the aggressor. This establishes a third position, eclipsing the split between good and bad, successful and failed, doer and done to, the deserving and the discarded.

The notion of "the third" functions as an antidote to splitting in Benjamin's work on social violence as well as within the analytic setting. "The third" refers to the ideals of lawful behavior and the union or solidarity of all persons. The concept carries with it the affirmation that every person has inalienable rights, and that there are actions that violate what is acceptable in terms of the treatment of others. This is a corollary of the dignity that all as humans possess. Further, in upholding the third, the witness confirms "all beings as part of the whole" (2014c). The social reality of human life is that we are connected to each other and fully interdependent. Whatever is done to one person is done to all. In this connection Benjamin refers to the traditional, pan-African ideal of *Ubuntu* (2014c; 2018, 234), as described in the work of the famous South African bishop, Desmond Tutu:

> A person is a person through other persons ... "my humanity is caught up, is inextricably bound up in yours." ... A person with *Ubuntu* ... has a proper self-assurance that comes from knowing that he or she belongs in a greater whole and is diminished when others are humiliated or diminished, when others are tortured or oppressed.
>
> (quoted in Benjamin 2014c)

The recent history of the West highlights the lesson that abstract ideals of law, universal rights, and morality are easily undermined through the inflammatory language of the "inhuman," "demonic" other. However, the element of "embodiment" gives a concreteness to the more abstract ideals of law and human connection. This is the difference between intellectually knowing something and actually feeling the truth or force of an insight, as it were, with one's whole body (Benjamin 2014a). It includes an identification with the suffering body of the injured, as well the dimension of the "rhythmic third," which Benjamin describes as "the empathic connection to others' suffering through the language of the body" (2014d; see also 2018, 224).

Victims

The victims of violence are devastated by the outside world's indifference and failure to stand forth as witnesses. A major insight by the breakthrough early psychoanalyst Sándor Ferenczi (1873–1933) was that when an event of trauma is ignored or denied by others, the victim feels as if the first trauma has been repeated (1988, xviii–xix, 193). Benjamin presents a similar proposition, that "bystanders appear—at least in the victim's mind—as virtually the same as perpetrators" (2014c). For her, Levi's *The Drowned and the Saved* suggests that the "experience of the failed witness is a central component of trauma" (2014b).

Lacking recognition, the victims may question whether the violent events they experienced have even occurred. They come to feel that their lives are of no value—dispensable. Victimized and degraded, they are often filled with shame. In their eyes they have been ostracized from the human community, and sometimes this actually occurs in terms of the attitudes of their neighbors and social group. Even the members of their family may believe that their loved ones have been "dishonored and demeaned" (Benjamin 2014c).

The effects of recognition withheld extend beyond the individuals' and families' feelings about themselves. The victims may attempt to escape or overcome the situation of powerlessness and rejection by identifying with the "powerful" perpetrator. This psychological reversal, through which the victim strives to become a perpetrator, feeds the cycle of violence. The ferocity of violence is intensified, because the victim both expects no help from the outside, and despairs of a world where the weak are denied access to laws and rights. Benjamin summarizes these repercussions: "When personal or collective trauma has been denied, the breakdown of lawfulness normalized, the victims are often pulled into oscillating assertions of doubt as to the importance of one's suffering and urges toward revenge" (2014c; see also 2018, 235).

Dignity is restored to the victims through authentic witnessing. Recognition liberates them from the fate of being cast off. As Benjamin expresses this,

> The suffering or death of the victims is thus dignified, their lives given value. Their lives are worthy of being mourned, as [Judith] Butler ... termed it, they are grievable lives. In other words, they are not simply objects to be discarded.
>
> (2014b)

More widely, true witnessing reinstates the notion of a human community of equally valued persons. The breach in this unity affects everyone, so that its repair has universal meaning. The effects include the affirmation of the "moral third," of a human world where the rule of law is upheld. These notions are further reinforced in cases where the victim has been given a public forum to protest and demand recognition—as in the TRC process: "The demand to be heard is reparative insofar as it affirms the principle that we are all human, that vulnerability and suffering must be honored and met with justice rather than disdained" (Benjamin 2014c; 2018, 239).

The consequences of active witnessing go beyond the restorative. Witnessing also gives agency to the victim,[4] who can themself become "a moral force" (Benjamin 2014c; 2018, 241). Drawing upon the recognition given, the victim may now feel enabled to extend compassion to others who have suffered. There is also the possibility to respond in forgiveness to the perpetrator, if, in the presence of social witnessing and solidarity (2014d), real efforts have been made by the perpetrator to admit guilt and by the community to repair the injury. Finally, when lawfulness and the moral third have been upheld, and communal solidarity renewed, the need for revenge can be foresworn and thus, the cycle of violence can be broken.

Perpetrators

A number of psychological features have been examined by Benjamin in relation to the impact of violence upon its actual agents. Perpetrators are often haunted by a feeling of having become alien to themselves. They see themselves as "monstrous," inhuman, contaminated by the blood on their hands (2014c). They may despair of rejoining their community, of re-establishing basic social relations as citizens and even as parents of children. Reacting to this dread, perpetrators justify their actions, calling upon the dictum of self-preservation, claiming that their case is one of the right to defend themselves, their family, and their community.

In harmony with the philosophy of South Africa's Truth and Reconciliation Commission,[5] Benjamin does not focus on the punishment of the offenders. She is concerned with acknowledgment, forgiveness, and repair, or with "restorative justice over prosecution" (2014c). A number of restorative possibilities are opened through particular features of recognition. Acknowledgement by the perpetrators of their responsibility for injuries to others, and with that the humanity of their victims, "may allow them to feel partially returned to themselves, to inhabit a human status in which their own vulnerability is included" (2014c). This may help them escape the pressing need to assert their dominance by overcoming the either/or of powerful or powerless, of invulnerable or vulnerable. Through the victim's forgiveness they can come to feel that their dignity has been restored and that they are once again part of the human community (2018, 243).

It is important to note the dramatic change from Benjamin's earlier works, especially the three books, in terms of the prominence now given to the notion of the individual's responsibility "for fellow human beings" (2014a). Benjamin articulates the responsibility for witnessing and healing the victim, and the responsibility for validating the solidarity of the community of humans and the reality of a moral universe. The failure of fulfilling such responsibility for others is also clear:

> The disavowal of public social responsibility for helping over harming is part of a complex process of withholding acknowledgment of injuries to victims in an unlawful world. This constitutes a form of failure to dignify suffering through witnessing that perpetuates breakdown of the moral third.
>
> (2014b)

In all, she annunciates a view that "responsibility for fellow human beings" (2018, 217) is a vital element in living a life of "dignity" (2014c) and authenticity (see also 2018, 246–248).

Concluding this section in a more critical vein, the power and pervasiveness of the concept of the moral third also brings to light difficulties in terms of public, everyday discourse. Especially in the context of those forums which Benjamin both participates in and cites—such as the South African Truth and Reconciliation Commission and the Israeli-Palestinian Acknowledgment Project—that include actual witnesses, victims, and perpetrators of social violence, the language about the moral third seems to me to be lifeless. Despite its obvious importance for Benjamin in addressing pressing episodes of injury and trauma, it is difficult to conceive that the terminology evokes passion, elicits action, or comforts.

There are perhaps traces of Benjamin's recognition of this problem in the writing itself. She acknowledges that the notion of the moral third has to be "emotionally grounded or embodied" (2018, 226) and not just appropriated as a type of principle. In this connection, as noted earlier, she adds the concept of the "rhythmic third" (224). Still, while the reference is to the suffering body of the other, this language, at least in the context of groups of witnesses, victims, and perpetrators, remains abstract and the terminology—rhythmic third—almost seems oxymoronic.

The emotional lacuna is most apparent in Benjamin's statement concerning the need to counter the potential witness's initial urge for "self-protection" in the face of episodes of suffering and trauma. She writes, "Overcoming this requires a *trust or belief in a form of the Third* that would make it possible to move beyond self-interest to identification with the Other" (2014a; my emphasis).

However, can the concept of the moral third engender "trust or belief"? There are some abstract ideas or ideals such as "*liberté, égalité, fraternité*," or democracy that have historical resonances and for which people have made sacrifices even of their lives. Many people have believed and even trusted in these, but the idea of the moral third does not share these resonances.

The most compelling account of the meaning of the moral third emerges when Benjamin refers to a "stunning paper," "The Dead Third," authored by Samuel Gerson (2009):

> [Gerson] took the experience of failed witnessing [in the wake of the Holocaust] to mean that the person or group feels that the social world that ought to care has disappeared and so the values of a caring world have become lifeless. Instead of recognition, there is only the unre-sponsiveness of *the heaven that does not weep*. Both the witnessing Other and the Third are dead.
>
> (2014b; my emphasis; 2018, 228)

As will be noted in Chapter 5, it is not accidental that Gerson's "stunning" statement utilizes religious rhetoric.

Individual trauma and the moral third

Benjamin's clinical work with the victims of individual trauma continued at the same time as she was addressing contemporary arenas of violence and collective trauma. Two crucial statements represent the personal and theoretical challenges that she was facing in that analytic context:

> I had not grasped yet that it required something outside the frame of what I then understood as psychoanalysis.
>
> (2018, 209)

I heard her [Jeannette] telling me that she needed me to embody *some* limit, some principle of right and wrong that I truly believed in, and that she could therefore believe in, too. This message from her was my first encounter in the context of violence with what I later came to formulate as the moral Third.

(211)

This section pursues a series of latent questions that explore the meaning, contexts, and ramifications for psychoanalysis of what she "came to formulate as the moral Third": What are the principal dimensions of the moral third? What is the developmental origin of an individual's sense of the moral third? Why is this concept "outside the frame of ... psychoanalysis"? Why is this "outside" required in the treatment of trauma? What is meant by Benjamin's realization that she needed to "embody" some features of this concept? Lastly, what is the new inside of psychoanalysis?

As we have seen, at a minimum the concept of the moral third refers to relationships or interactions that are governed by justice, fairness, and, in particular, lawfulness. Its importance and complexity is best explored through its two facets, that is, the moral third refers to both a "mental position" and "interpersonal processes" (225). As expressed by Benjamin,

I use the term Moral Third to refer both to the mental position and the interpersonal processes that enable the repair of such breakdowns in lawfulness through dialogue, mutual understanding or atonement. Holding the tension between Is and Ought, this mental position opposes denial which collapses that distinction. It affirms what is lawful even in its absence; it affirms the value of acknowledging the truth of violations even when they cannot be undone.

(225)

The moral third is, first, a "mental position" that includes underlying "values, rules and principles" of lawfulness (Benjamin 2009, 442). The moral third, second, involves specific "interpersonal processes," that is, actions including "dialogue, mutual understanding or atonement" that facilitate "repair." Since the principles are the theoretical basis for the actions, they will be explored here initially. A discussion of the processes will then follow. However, the relationship between these two components of the moral third is dynamic. The interpersonal processes themselves can come to demonstrate or even develop "faith" in the principles. Additionally, the principles are first experienced or created, "primordially," within the mother–infant dyad (2007, 22).

The moral third: principles

Lawfulness, the dominant characteristic of the moral third, is somewhat conventionally described by Benjamin as the "principle of right and wrong" (2018, 211). In a similar vein, the moral third is defined as "the principle whereby we create relationships in accord with ethical values" (2012, 98). More specifically, the overall principles of the moral third are: "respect for human dignity" (2018, 51), acknowledgment of human vulnerability (2014c), responsibility "for fellow human beings" (2014a), affirmation that "suffering must be honored and met with justice" (2018, 239), and the inclusiveness, interdependence, and union of the human community (2016b, 16).

It is important to Benjamin that the notion of the moral third is not limited to specific societies and historical periods. It refers to a moral order that is universal. However, while this order may be in principle universal, it does not always reign. The world often "offers" violence, torture, and killing. Part of the substance of the moral third can be revealed by what it relentlessly contests, "what is wrong, what should never happen to a child, to a human being" (2018, 213). However, once again, this trust "affirms what is lawful even in its absence; it affirms the value of acknowledging the truth of violations even when they cannot be undone" (225).

The moral third: interpersonal processes

The notion of lawfulness, in the sense of justice, fairness, honesty, and sincerity, spans the presentation of those interpersonal processes that manifest the moral third. Benjamin's discussion of these usually envisions a particular context, the clinical arena and the inevitable cycles of rupture and repair that punctuate the treatment of individual trauma (2012, 126). More specifically, the analyst's acts of equality, mutuality, asymmetry, responsibility, and surrender prominently portray the intersubjective processes of the moral third.

"Rupture and repair" refers to the breakdowns that interrupt progress in ongoing clinical work. The breakdowns occur as especially difficult issues arise in the dialogue. They result from dissociated feelings and experiences, injuries, and vulnerabilities in the life of the patient and/or the therapist. A conflict ensues with alternative shame and blame passed between the players of this serious game. Caught in this web, the only escape is through making contact with the moral third and its underlying sense of fairness and justice. For Benjamin, "the moral third depends upon acknowledgment of disruptions, disappointments, violations of expectancy, and more broadly upon acknowledgment of injuries and trauma that challenge principles of fairness, and respect for dignity" (2018, 51).

While repair is never final, each instance reinforces trust in the processes that represent the moral third. Equality and some associated ideals are characteristics that Benjamin incorporates into her description of an "egalitarian" centered psychoanalysis. In her words,

> In calling this the *moral third*, I am suggesting that clinical practice may ultimately be founded in certain values, such as the acceptance of

uncertainty, humility, and compassion that form the basis of a demo-
cratic or egalitarian view of psychoanalytic process.

(2004, 34)

Mutuality and asymmetry are two other features of this clinical lawfulness.
Mutuality encompasses the truth that the dialogue is a shared process. It
is not a relationship of subject and object, but of two partners listening,
learning, and developing together. Mutuality also extends to the notion
that the relationship is not between an all-knowing, objective healer and a
damaged, ailing patient. Both individuals bring their own vulnerabilities,
memories, and feelings to the joint encounter (Benjamin 2018, 103–109).
However, the quality of asymmetry also applies here. This is most evident
in the particular responsibilities that the therapist has that do not apply to
the patient. These include the honest acknowledgment that in the pursuit
of the patient's health, the latter is brought to re-experience moments of
violence, guilt, pain, and trauma. The psychoanalyst is also responsible for
what Benjamin terms "surrender." She means by this that in the midst of
a breakdown in the dialogue, it is the therapist's responsibility to acknowledge what is happening, and to confess their active part in the push and
pull of blaming. This situation is well reviewed in the following:

> I also think of this as the *moral third*—reachable only through this
> experience of taking responsibility for bearing pain and shame. In
> taking such responsibility, the analyst is putting an end to the buck
> passing the patient has always experienced—that is, to the game of
> ping-pong wherein each member of the dyad tries to put the bad into
> the other. The analyst says, in effect, "I'll go first." In orienting to the
> moral third of responsibility, the analyst is also demonstrating the
> route out of helplessness.
>
> (2004, 33)

Inside the mother–infant dyad

The significance of the interaction between mother, or other primary
caregiver(s), and infant is a centerpiece of many post-Freudian streams
in psychoanalysis. It is especially crucial in the Object Relations school
and those associated with the more contemporary relational development. Benjamin's stance within Relational Psychoanalysis as well as her
vital commitment and contribution to feminist perspectives ensure that the
mother-infant dyad has a primary, "primordial" role in her presentation of
the moral third. She movingly speaks of the importance of her "practical
personal experiences as a mother": "A mother, I should add, who studied
mother–infant interaction and before that was passionately involved in the
second wave generation of feminism, which sought to change the relations
of mothering and working as well as psychoanalytic theory" (2018, 2).
A fuller understanding of the moral third thus requires the examination of

this period of dyadic experiences. It could be said that all of the features of the moral third, as well as the third itself, are prefigured and first developed in the variety of subtle, pre-symbolic, i.e., pre-linguistic, exchanges between mother and infant.

The expectation of justice or lawfulness originates out of the mother's overall pattern of attentive and caring actions, as well as her supportive response in times when these are absent. Benjamin writes, "Relational repair ... involves the caregiver acknowledging—in deeds and communicative gestures—the violations of expected patterns of soothing or responsiveness. This process of repair serves to create a sense of the *lawful world*, a central category of experience" (2018, 6). At the other end of this modest beginning are the adult's witnessing, acknowledgment, and repair in response to those who suffer injustice in far-off lands (236).

The reverberations of failures in the mother's attentive and caring actions can be, unsurprisingly, traumatic. They may undermine the basic trust in the mother, in the self, and in the world. Of course, such failures would have to be extremely serious, either in terms of the emotional intensity and even possible violence felt by the infant, or in terms of unstable actions by the caregiver that undercut the infant's expectation of helpful responses. In such cases the infant may feel that the mother is missing, collapsed, or somehow destroyed by the infant's (imaginary) aggression.

Revolutionary studies in infant development over the past four or five decades have given prominence to the manner that both mutuality, as in episodes of play, and asymmetry pulse through the life of the mother–infant dyad (Benjamin 2018, 73–75). In the relationship of signaling and responding to each other, both are empowered. Still, the mother obviously has responsibilities that define the asymmetry. These include attention to the infant's needs, watching and encouraging development, and the aforementioned issue of surrender. Benjamin provides palpable examples of the mother's surrender to the infant's needs rather than her just reluctantly giving-in within some type of battle of wills, writing,

> Recognizing both her own need and the baby's need as legitimate, but knowing whose need comes first, allows the mother to relate to the baby's cry in the middle of the night not as a persecutory experience of being "done to," submitting to the tyrant baby, but as a necessary condition.
>
> (83)

Benjamin adds that moments of mutuality and play with the infant are important for the mother's feeling that the relationship is not just about self-sacrifice (2018, 84). In her words, "The 'reward' of accommodating the needs of her little partner is that the mother can share in states of high affective intensity, joyfulness, play as well as feel able to comfort and soothe" (84).

Exploring the frame

A number of issues are embedded in Benjamin's statement that the moral third is "outside the frame of what I then understood as psychoanalysis" (2018, 209). How did she understand the prior psychoanalytic "frame"? Do all the dimensions of the moral third emanate from this outside, or only some? Finally, why did she find that this outside was required by psychoanalysis?

There are a few relevant references in Benjamin's work to the disciplinary boundaries between psychoanalysis and both philosophy and political science. As we will see, one perspective on the way that the moral third breaks out of the limits of psychoanalysis appears in relation to these areas. In *Like Subjects, Love Objects* (1995) she replies to a philosopher criticizing her treatment of the theory of recognition, "Here the distinction between a philosophical and a psychoanalytic register may be of some use" (20). The philosopher, J. Meehan, seems to have argued that Benjamin's concept of "recognition," that there is a need and desire to recognize the other as a distinct person in their own right and to be recognized in turn, is a "normative ideal" (20). A normative ideal is prescriptive; the label implies that something is a moral good. Benjamin responds that recognition concerns a feature of natural human development, an "empirical possibility and necessity of development" (20), that may or may not be realized in any specific case. She adds, "when we postulate a psychological *need* (not a social need or a normative ideal) for recognition, we mean that failure to satisfy the need will inevitably result in difficulties or even damage to the psyche" (21). Benjamin insists that she is not going beyond the developmental and "empirical" by including or addressing a "social need"—what is good for society—or a "normative ideal"—what is morally right for persons. A later work, "The Discarded and the Dignified," briefly reaffirms her position by stating that the essay will not take up philosophical issues:

> The question as to the responsibility of individuals who are not directly implicated in violence and suffering but nonetheless informed of it daily by the media is not one that I intend to take up philosophically. There are many ethical questions implied in such a notion of witnessing ... relating to how and whether attention is paid. My scope here is limited to the question of the psychological forces in play.
>
> (2014a)

From the first page to the last, a vastly different tone is struck in *Beyond Doer and Done To* (2018).[6] Benjamin issues a challenge to the earlier demarcated branches of knowledge; "I hope that these propositions ['broadly to our entire view of human development and social bonds'] will reach across the disciplinary barriers and enable non-psychoanalysts to access the social and philosophical implications of intersubjective psychoanalysis" (1). The specific issues Benjamin has in mind concern addressing injustice, oppression, violence, and trauma suffered by the most vulnerable. In her words,

> From the standpoint of psychoanalytic recognition theory, I would argue that efforts to think about repairing the world and restoring the Third require a psychological understanding, too often spurned by philosophical and political theory, of the effects of collective trauma ... in relation to harming and suffering, power and helplessness, humiliation and indignity.
>
> (246)

Additionally, Benjamin confirms that this clarion call for social and individual justice is integrally tied to what she sees as her (new) psychoanalytic position, to "the matter of creating or repairing the moral Third, as in the idea of repairing the world or moral community" (239). In this, she unambiguously includes notions of what is a moral good for individuals and societies within the parameters of psychoanalysis.

Still, a number of features of thirdness and the moral third, especially within the domain of the interpersonal processes, are already deeply rooted in the history as well as the current theory and practice of psychoanalysis, and thus not outside the older psychoanalytic frame. For the last two decades, conceptions of the third and thirdness have animated the writings of psychoanalysts who insist that "analytic practice involves processes and phenomena that transcend the boundaries of a single mind" (Gerson 2004). To speak of these processes theorists utilize varieties of terminology including triangulation, analytic field, a third position, the analytic third, developmental third, cultural third, relational third, as well as Benjamin's "one in the third" (2018, 30), rhythmic third, symbolic third, and moral third.

Benjamin regularly acknowledges a debt to earlier analysts in discussions of the central "interpersonal processes" within the moral third. Ferenczi is cited by her for his commitment to the equality within the analytic dyad, and especially for his view of the repetition of trauma that healing necessitates. Benjamin reflects, "Here I have come increasingly to value the bravely prescient contributions of Ferenczi, which emphasized how productively we can (and must) use repetitions of trauma caused by our failures as well as difficulties tolerating our own feelings and reactions" (2012, 128). D. W. Winnicott is often featured in her explanation of surrender: "The idea that the lawful third develops through acknowledging violations expands the Winnicottian idea of survival of destruction" (128). Daniel Stern's transformational infant research is credited with opening up our understanding of the dynamics of the mother-infant dyad. As an example, Benjamin acknowledges his contributions spanning "early infancy studies and later a general theory of mind, [that] formulated the process of recognition in terms of the need for intersubjective orientation and relatedness, which are necessary for their own sake" (2018, 9).

Benjamin is equally magnanimous in detailing the contributions of contemporary psychoanalysts who advanced the understanding of these interpersonal processes. A few among countless others that she references are Malcolm Slavin, Lewis Aron, and Donna Orange. In one instance, a clinical episode between Slavin and a patient is introduced to illustrate the importance of self-acknowledgment as part of the therapist's practice. He was brought to acknowledge his own vulnerabilities, and the difficulty he felt in fully opening himself up to the depth of his patient's despair, while also knowing the importance of that for real progress to be made (Benjamin 2018, 62–63). Aron, who co-authored work with Benjamin, is referenced in conjunction with presenting the dynamic between mutuality and asymmetry. This is the major focus of his book *A Meeting of Minds: Mutuality in Psychoanalysis*. Lastly, while Benjamin frequently reviews her disagreement with Orange over the pertinence of mutual recognition in clinical practice (37–38), she commends the latter's sensitive efforts to witness the suffering and trauma of both her patients and the oppressed throughout the world (2010).

Opening the frame

Clearly, as we have just seen, those elements of the moral third that Benjamin labels "interpersonal processes" are legitimately situated within the historical and contemporary frame of the discipline of psychoanalysis. The disciplinary breakthrough is announced through the nomenclature of the moral third itself, as well as some of the features she characterizes as its values or principles. Benjamin's paragraph-long defense of the term "moral" is an indicator that something is being proposed that at least some analysts find alarming.

> Ironically the sense of the term *moral third* was lost on some analysts, especially traditional ones, who imagined a superego driven analyst imposing moral judgment on the patient. In fact the concept of thirdness is the antithesis of coercive imposition of one subjectivity or set of ideals over the other insofar as it denotes the creation of space for recognizing and negotiating difference. My use of the word *moral* is meant to invoke a sense of lawfulness based on respect for the other's reality and subjectivity, thus countering the "my way versus your way" of complementary power relations. The theory of the moral third relates to understanding how recognition of the other's equal dignity and value but different perspective and subjectivity develops as an emotional experience with others not simply as an abstract idea.
>
> (2012, 124)

This defense of the term "moral" in "moral third" reveals the uneasiness of "traditional" psychoanalysts and others with Benjamin's crucial concept. A defining feature of Freudian psychoanalysis is the view that treatment of neuroses requires a judgment-free environment. Part of the problem that the analyst faces is the patient's own rejection and repression of feelings, memories, and experiences conventionally viewed as immoral and evil. In Freud's classical "structural model" of the psyche, the superego is that harsh, unrelenting, moralistic force behind these processes. Benjamin argues that the "moral third" refers to the principle of "the other's equal dignity and value" rather than the "coercive imposition of one subjectivity or set of ideals over the other." She makes the same point a little later in the text in relation to the term ethical, that is, that bringing the ethical into practice does not involve the "imposition of morality" (2012, 129).

Yet, this defense does not do full justice to the wider dimensions of the moral third, which are important sources of its power to address both individual and collective trauma. Benjamin frequently uses the evocative terms "trust," "belief," and even "faith" in conjunction with the moral third to describe the sense of lawfulness that the analyst brings to the patient. Here are some examples:

> Overcoming this requires a trust or belief in a form of the Third that would make it possible to move beyond self-interest to identification with the Other (2014a);
> believing in a lawful world, the moral intersubjective third (2012, 127);
> [the] sense of lawfulness and faith in a moral third (129);
> I'm reaching for something [Michael] Eigen has called the area of faith. ... Somewhere, this primordial thirdness joins up with moral thirdness—witnessing, attuning to and recognizing psychic pain—which is directly related to faith.
>
> (2007, 22)

This "faith" in the moral third has both an interpersonal aspect, i.e., between persons, and what legitimately might be called a metaphysical or transcendental dimension. The emphasis on human behavior and solidarity is seen in Benjamin's statement, "The mental representation of lawful world refers not to juridical law, but to a belief in the value and possibility of intelligible, responsive and respectful behavior as a condition of mental sanity and interpersonal/social bonds" (2018, 6).

However, Benjamin's discussion of thirdness and the moral third at times reaches beyond the human community to other living beings. One aspect of this she considers is in reference to studies of animal behavior, in this instance, fireflies. She believes that it is not too much to suggest that there is a "transcendental or transpersonal force," an "organic imperative," "inherent in the process of sharing signals, in all communication." Such human processes as "attunement or recognition" can be seen to exemplify this phenomenon (2007, 16).[7]

The transcendental, metaphysical, (even what might be termed) religious character of the moral third sometimes emerges. Benjamin writes,

"I began originally to think of the Third as related to an original sense of harmony that exists both in the world and self, an idea one might find in neo-Platonic mysticism" (2018, 21). She continues by referring to ideas of Søren Kierkegaard in terms of holding on to the Third and surrendering to the Third (21), by which Kierkegaard means surrendering to God (Kierkegaard 1995, 103, 107). There is also an earlier discussion by Benjamin of Kierkegaard, where she quotes another analyst (Marie Hoffman): "The third, which thinkers would call the idea, is the true, the good, or more accurately the God relationship" (Benjamin 2012, 124). This wider sentiment is also evoked in an allusion to the mother-infant dyad: "Likewise, the energetic, rhythmic aspect of the nascent third informs the moral third, it is the music of universal laws and meaning" (2007, 16). As will be explained below, this feature of the moral third is not just some type of poetic exuberance. The trust, faith, or belief in a transcendent lawfulness, "a larger principle of necessity, rightness, goodness" (9), is absolutely vital to the possibility of repair through the moral third.

It should be noted that despite Benjamin's references in *Beyond Doer and Done To* to "neo-Platonic mysticism" and Kierkegaard (2018, 21), she maintains a very disparaging attitude toward religion or at least biblical religions. For example, immediately preceding the important statement that Jeannette told her about the need to "embody ... some principle of right and wrong," Benjamin writes that, "I did, however, think about how Jeannette had grown up in a world surrounded by useless religious 'moral' authorities who offered discipline and punishment, whose ideas of right and wrong were absolute and disconnected from felt experience" (211). While this statement might seem to be a straightforward report about her patient's experience, it patently reflects Benjamin's own evaluation of religion as presented in both earlier and recent works. In *The Bonds of Love*, references to the Grand Inquisitor scene in Dostoyevsky's *The Brothers Karamazov*, and to the classic bondage novel *The Story of O*, correlate religion with the illusionary promise of redemption in exchange for the believer's complete submission to absolute authority (1988, 5, 60).[8]

Another feature that Benjamin associates with religion is the splitting between the dignified and the discarded, a theme discussed in the prior section of this chapter. In *Beyond Doer and Done To*, she refers to "the Cain and Abel myth" as "the original myth of 'Only one can live'" (2018, 230). This view is elaborated in an earlier work,

> We must confront the equally powerful implication of this early myth that only one child was chosen, and in other cases, that those who perished were not grieved, not respected, not prayed for; or that their loss was due to weakness and abjection; or that those who died were not favored or, to the contrary, were victims of envy.
>
> (2014b)

Thus, the Cain and Abel story represents the "rejection of the third" (2014b). The divine preference for Abel over Cain illustrates the notion "that only one child was chosen" (2014b) and the other was unworthy and, with justification, had to be abandoned and discarded. For Benjamin, the biblical text, "this first myth of progeny" (2014b), gives a divine imprimatur to the psychological splitting—violence—victimization, as well as the self-justification and triumphalism that haunt human struggles (2018, 232).

Although not directly stated, Benjamin is articulating a familiar sentiment, that religion, particularly biblical religions, are psychologically dysfunctional as well as innately absolutist and exclusivist. Religion enshrines the notion that there can only be one truth and one path to salvation. God stands on the side of the righteous and ultimately victorious, and everyone else perpetuates evil, falsehood, and death. While there is more than a little evidence to support Benjamin's associations, all religions also exhibit more expansive, supportive, and pluralist currents, and in Chapter 4 we will see some vivid expressions of this in the works of some modern Jewish philosophers.

Contexts and significance of the moral third

It is illuminating to now return to the context for Benjamin's insight that she needed to find "something outside the frame of what I then understood as psychoanalysis" (2018, 209). As quoted earlier, Benjamin explains,

> I heard her [Jeannette] telling me that she needed me to embody *some* limit, some principle of right and wrong that I truly believed in, and that she could therefore believe in, too. This message from her was my first encounter in the context of violence with what I later came to formulate as the moral Third.
>
> (211)

The treatment of a patient suffering from a traumatic past is the situation that eventually leads Benjamin to the formulation of the moral third, that "principle of right and wrong." Another patient in an analogous state confirms this message when she describes how Benjamin was able to help her: "Hannah explicitly articulated this meaning in her own language sometime later when she said that what I had given her was a moral universe" (161).

Overall, there are two contexts in which Benjamin feels compelled to draw upon the concept of the moral third. Both concern the treatment of trauma, one personal and especially developmental, and the other historical or collective. The two patients above suffered from developmental trauma, that is, either some specific episodes of violence in their early years or the severe lack of an attentive and caring environment, what is called "empathic failures" (2018, 91). The consequences of developmental trauma are very well detailed by Benjamin. There is a deep and abiding loss of trust and confidence in the caregiver, but beyond this, the self, the future, and the world themselves are felt to be forsaken.

What is required for repair is trust, belief, or faith in some critical principles of the moral third. There must be acknowledgment of injustice, that something is wrong and that it "warrants repair" (Benjamin 2018, 88), that is, that real pain and suffering have occurred, and they must be redressed. This latter begins with a confirmation of the dignity and worthiness of the one in distress (89). There also is a need for a "lawful world" (6), or what Hannah described as a trust in a "moral universe" (161).

Benjamin sees deep ties in the understanding and treatment between individual and collective trauma, particularly in the sense of what has been lost and what repair necessitates (2012, 129). In her words,

> I have come to see the link between our action in the consultation room and the broader vision of becoming an active bystander that makes humans socially responsible, empowered to witness if not to change and thus to recognize pain and affirm the dignity of those who suffer.
>
> (129)

Embodiment

There is a final feature in Benjamin's construction of the moral third within the clinical context that still needs to be addressed. It consists in her awareness that repair requires more than the description or expression of those principles of the moral third. "I heard her [Jeannette] telling me that she needed me to embody *some* limit, some principle of right and wrong that I truly believed in, and that she could therefore believe in, too" (2018, 211). What does it mean for these to be embodied and why is this necessary?

Technically, embodiment concerns emphatic identification with the other (Benjamin 2018, 227), passionately described from the point of view of the sufferer: "In witnessing, this other mind now resonates with the vibration of my pain: we are together in the rhythmicity of the Third" (12). However, in light of the experiences of the different victims, this often presents a profound, terrifying personal challenge for the analyst. Benjamin speaks of what this trial entails: "If I could be a healer who in some way did know about life and death, knew such terrible things could happen"; "Yet to be a witness, not to fail, to try to embrace this knowledge—it seemed I was obliged to try my best" (211). Both sides recognize that the presence of the other is crucial; repair cannot be done solely by the self. For the victim, "something else had to happen, but she [Jeannette] did not let herself think that the something else had to do with me [Benjamin], with something the Other alone can do" (209).

There are a number of features that the other can give, in another sense, that both can create and share.[9] These include a sense of safety— "The dimension evoked by the images of warmth and space and firm ground beneath suggests to me both safety and surrender, not only the differentiating aspect of the lawful world but its harmony" (Benjamin 2018, 212)—and the affirmation of the sufferer's dignity and worth— "The sense of self-cohesion (being), the worthiness of self and other, and the experience of agency are united through the reliability of caring others" (89). Also required is the belief that despite the injustice which has occurred there is a universal lawfulness or justice that can be drawn upon (213, 216).

Thus, in confronting traumatized persons, Benjamin finds that she is tasked with witnessing to some fundamental—I am arguing universal, transcendental, metaphysical, almost religious—principles. These concern the union of the human community, and the nature and meaning of life itself. To be effective these cannot just be known by the patient. Healing requires that there is belief in, faith in, trust in them. This in turn demands that the clinician testify herself through actions—knowing terrible things, witnessing devastating injury, acknowledging injustice, and together working-through repair.

Conclusion: the new "Inside" of psychoanalysis

Of course, this insight and development in Jessica Benjamin's work is not an isolated event, especially in the context of contemporary psycho-analysis. Much of the background and possible ramifications of what has been termed the ethical turn in psychoanalysis is detailed in *The Ethical Turn: Otherness and Subjectivity in Contemporary Psychoanalysis* (2016), edited by David Goodman and Eric Severson. They underscore the work of the philosopher Emmanuel Levinas and the focus on one's responsi-bility to the suffering other. There are many other factors in the emerging emphasis on ethics as "first psychology" (i), including the intersubjective or relational model of human life, which is encapsulated by Stephen Mitchell: "An individual human mind is an oxymoron; subjectivity always develops in the context of intersubjectivity" (2000, 57). The prominence of the relationship between mother and infant is noted in Hans Loewald's address of 1978, "The Waning of the Oedipus Complex," commenting about "the contemporary decline of psychoanalytic interest in the oedipal phase and oedipal conflicts and the predominance of interest and research in pre-oedipal development, in the mother–infant dyad" (2000, 386). The increasing psychoanalytic concern with meaning as a funda-mental constituent of a full human life is portrayed by Mitchell: "What the patient needs is not a rational reworking of unconscious infantile fan-tasies ... [but] a revitalization and expansion of his own capacity to gen-erate experience that feels real, meaningful, and valuable" (1993, 24). He adds that "the term meaningful here refers to a sense of personal value, importance, and devotion" (234). The attention to traumatic experiences, so important to Benjamin, is widespread. Donna Orange's description of psychological compassion brings together some of these factors, writing that this approach is an implicitly interpretative process of giving lived meaning and dignity to a shattered person's life by enabling integration of the pain and loss as opposed to dissociation or fragmentation. ... [It] says to every patient: your suffering is human suffering, and when the bell tolls for you, it also tolls for me.

(2016, 57)

What, then, is the legacy for psychoanalysis of Benjamin's formulation of the moral third? In an earlier work, the last book in her influential triad on relationality and recognition, Benjamin surveyed what the founder of psychoanalysis had contributed and what she calculated was the cost. She wrote,

This essay, therefore, will query psychoanalysis, concentrating on the ambivalent legacy Freud bequeathed us, a kind of liberation, freedom from religious and moral strictures, from grand ideals, from the temptation to save and redeem—but offered at a price: denial of the analyst's subjectivity and desire which might mirror that of the patient; distance from the helpless, the passive, and for that matter, the feminine Other, identification with whom did not always come easily to Freud, did not fit with his notion of objectivity and science.

(1998, 5)

One way of reading Benjamin's latest work is that she is now questioning whether psychoanalysis can continue to live with that earlier described "liberation," even beyond the issue of its lamentable price. At the time of the quotation, she found that Freud's gift, while it was still compelling, had a troubling cost. The reappropriation of that "cost," "denial of the analyst's subjectivity and desire that might mirror that of the patient; distance from the helpless, the passive, and for that matter, the feminine Other," became an important feature of Relational Psychoanalysis. However, at this later moment, in conjunction with the deepening encounter with both individual and collective trauma, Benjamin realizes that the liberation—in a wider sense, since it is not about conventional strictures—is itself seriously flawed. As we have seen, she recognizes a fundamental dimension of her task today precisely in terms of the commitment to universal and moral principles, grand ideals, and, most of all, the responsibility to witness and repair, all of which—"outside the [prior] frame of ... psychoanalysis"— constitute the "moral third".

Notes

1 The concept of "the third" has a wide variety of meanings in psychoanalysis. Samuel Gerson describes three different uses of the term in the literature:

For some, this something called a third that transcends individualities is thought of as a product of an interaction between persons ["the relational third"]; others speak of it as a context that originates apart from us even as it binds us together ["the cultural third"]; and there are some for whom the third is a developmental achievement that creates a location permitting reflective observation of lived experience, be it singular or communal ["the developmental third"].

(2004, 65)

All nine articles in this 2004 issue of the *Psychoanalytic Quarterly* were dedicated to examining the history and concept of the third in psychoanalytic theory and practice.

2   The main resource for the discussion of collective trauma is Benjamin's presentation of 2014, "The Discarded and the Dignified," Parts 1–6 (2014a, 2014b, 2014c, 2014d), which I find is her most comprehensive examination of these relations. She takes up these issues again in her latest, more available venue, *Beyond Doer and Done To* (2018). I will note several places from the latter where similar insights are found to the 2014 presentation, as well as incorporate specific insights that augment the earlier examination.

3   This is the feminist critic Julia Kristeva's term for the despised, expelled part of the self that is projected upon the other (1982).

4   In her first book, Benjamin expresses the link between recognition and agency, "Recognition is that response from the other which makes meaningful the feelings, intentions, and actions of the self. It allows the self to realize its agency and authorship in a tangible way" (1988, 12).

5   The TRC was given the power of "granting amnesty to individuals in exchange for a full disclosure relating to the crime for which amnesty was being sought" (Tutu 1999, 30).

6   In calling for the need to reach across disciplinary boundaries (2018, 1), Benjamin refers to her earlier article "Intersubjectivity" (2016a).

7   Still, this consideration about animal behavior has a long history within psychoanalysis, starting with Freud and his reflections on the two drives, *eros* and *thanatos*, that are exhibited in all life-forms. Benjamin herself mentions in the above discussion the work of the psychoanalyst Louis Sander (2007, 16).

8   See the more detailed analysis of Benjamin's view of religion in the author's *Contemporary Psychoanalysis and Modern Jewish Philosophy* (Oppenheim 2017, 66–67).

9   Orange notes that in responding to the other's suffering, one may be able to give—peace, trust, faith—something that oneself did not previously possess. In her words, "Something happens to me in the face of the other's need so that my giving has the quality of participating" (2011, 51).

2 Psychological perspectives on trust and trauma

The fundamental trust in the self, others, and the world constitutes the very basis of the human psyche. It is the platform for all endeavor, without which human life itself is impossible. Despite this centrality, the elements or features of this trust are quite enigmatic. The phenomenon of psychic trauma is one type of lens that brings to prominence crucial features of trust. If trust is the scaffolding for life, trauma instigates its collapse. The dynamic between trust and trauma is mutually illuminating, particularly featured in those processes that psychologists combine under the rubric of recovery.

This chapter begins by detailing Erikson's analysis of basic trust, including its genesis in the mother-infant dyad and its relation to both hope and religion. Herman's and Van der Kolk's works are explored for their research on trauma's perplexing symptoms and some tested programs of repair. After augmenting the discussion with relevant reflections from a few contemporary psychoanalysts, the examination concludes by outlining the parallels between Erikson's exposition and crucial insights of the other interlocutors.

Erikson and basic trust

While the psychoanalyst Erik H. Erikson is best known for his analysis of adolescent identity, his examination of the initial "ego strength" (1964, 165), basic trust, is itself a staple of psychological investigations of human development. "Basic Trust vs. Basic Mistrust" is the first stage in Erikson's classic eight-stage psychosocial diagram of development. In this he follows and transforms Sigmund Freud's famous psychosexual scheme of stages: Oral, Anal, Phallic, Latent, and Genital. Erikson widens the scope from Freud's physiological and psychological focus and also lengthens the purview beyond the stage of sexual maturity to that of the fullness of human life. The eight stages are: Basic Trust vs. Basic Mistrust, Autonomy vs. Shame and Doubt, Initiative vs. Guilt, Industry vs. Inferiority, Identity vs. Role Diffusion, Intimacy vs. Isolation, Generativity vs. Stagnation, and Ego Integrity vs. Despair (1997, 56–57).[1]

There are a number of guiding principles within Erikson's scheme. The stages coalesce around what he terms "crises," which reflect new constellations of physiological, psychological, and social factors, and build upon the outcomes of what preceded. As the individual develops through infancy, childhood, adolescence, adulthood, and old age, changes in the body (soma), the mind (psyche), and the social environment (ethos) mark developmental challenges and turning points. In Erikson's words, "A human being, thus, is at all times an organism, an ego, and a member of society and is involved in all three processes of organization" (1963, 36). The widening of social players is one of the most important elements that differentiates this plan from Freud's, carefully detailing the movement of the individual's involvement with others from the mother, through the family, school, friends, colleagues, and intimate partner, to the contemporary world and the whole human historical presence. The changing challenge or conflict within each stage is noted through the presence of the term "versus." Success is not envisioned as complete or final. The ego strengths continue to evolve, building upon the past and developing through the future. Erikson writes,

> What the child acquires at a given stage is a certain *ratio* between the positive and the negative which, if the balance is toward the positive, will help him to meet later crises with a predisposition toward the sources of vitality.
>
> (1968, 325)

Lastly, and a feature often undervalued in descriptions of Erikson's work, is the interpersonal or intersubjective dimension.[2] For Erikson, the dynamic between persons, starting with mother and infant, is absolutely crucial to understanding human life. It is not just that persons require some requisite support or collaboration from others, but that personal engagement is the *sine qua non* for the quality of life and maturity of both sides. This insight comes across through Erikson's notion of "mutual activation":

> *Mutual activation* is the crux of the matter; for human ego strength, while employing all means of testing reality, depends from stage to stage upon a network of mutual influences within which the person actuates others even as he is actuated, and within which the person is "inspired with active properties," even as he so inspires others.
>
> (1963, 165)

As indicated above, Erikson's description of the decisive outcome of the first stage of life is a trust in the self, in others, and in the world. He provides a good overview in the statement,

> For the most fundamental prerequisite of mental vitality, I have already nominated a *sense of basic trust*, which is a pervasive attitude

toward oneself and the world derived from the experiences of the first year of life. By "trust" I mean an essential trustfulness of others as well as a fundamental sense of one's own trustworthiness.

(1968, 96)

In terms of the self or ego, this can be put in condensed form as an abiding sense of an inner integrity. Confirmed through the attitude and behavior of others, and immediate introspection, the individual carries an inner feeling of unity, consistency, and separateness. All of this is well expressed by Erikson as "confidence that somehow in the midst of change, one has an inner sameness and continuity which others can recognize and which is so certain that it can be taken for granted" (quoted in Schlein 2016, 160).

Two other vital features that comprise the sense of basic trust in the self are the feeling of one's essential goodness and the affect of self-love. What is particularly significant about these is that, as with all of the elements of basic trust, they first emerge from the interaction of the baby with the primary caregiver or caregivers. Thus, this sense of inner goodness and the attitude of self-love, while "taken for granted," are not innate. Goodness and self-love are given to and carried by the infant, as it were, because the m/other regards the infant as both good and lovable.[3]

The mother or maternal caregiver represents the social dimension in this initial psychosocial stage, actually as both trusted other and, as will be addressed later, the world. Her pervasive presence in the portrayal of basic trust is underscored by a surprising acknowledgement that Erikson communicated to Stephen Schlein, who was writing a book about his teacher. Erikson remarked that he originally wanted to label the first stage as "inner confidence," but his wife, the psychologist Joan Erikson, corrected him, "No Erik, inner confidence does not capture the complexity of the mother–infant interaction, and what the baby receives from the mother … the first stage of life ought to be called 'basic trust'" (quoted in Schlein 2016, 15). Undoubtedly the notion of "inner confidence" may convey some of the elements of the trust in the self, but it neither advances an understanding of trust in others and world, nor, as Joan Erikson affirmed, elevates the full dimensions of those foundational experiences within the mother–infant dyad.

While taking care of the baby's physical requirements, such as nourishment and hygiene, are obviously important, Erikson stresses the ultimate significance of the quality of maternal care. The mother's "messages" to the infant are communicated subtly, somatically through all the senses, in feeding, handling, speaking, and playing. Being attuned to the infant's needs and responding in essentially consistent and predictable ways communicates that the self can be trusted, i.e., that these needs are genuine, and that other persons can be relied on to respond to legitimate physical and emotional appeals. The mother's loving responses also reflect the "true recognition of the child *as hers and as good*" (1964, 120; my emphasis). Erikson is particularly aware of the role of the mother's face as confirming the separateness and integrity of the infant, while at the same time laying the foundation for some of those later encounters between self and others that are so intense as to appear to eclipse physical boundaries. He writes that this primary relationship "assures us, ever again, of *separateness transcended* and yet also of *distinctiveness confirmed*, and thus of the very basis of a sense of 'I'" (1997, 45).

The examination of the mother–infant relation points beyond the gifts that the infant receives. The mother's generative care of the infant confirms, or perhaps even creates, her own attributes of loving, being responsible, and being a provider of firm and sensitive guidance. This dynamic is the paradigmatic example of mutual activation. Erikson is also insistent that maternal care requires more than a single, isolated individual or even couple. Mothers must draw upon the wider community and culture for the social verification of their role of bringing up children, and for the specific values and meanings that must be passed on to the infant (1964, 116, 142).

Finally, the fullness of trust goes beyond the self, and m/other. There is an indirect but significant cosmic dimension, as it were, to the information conveyed to the infant through the mother's loving care. Just as the mother represents the universe for her child,[4] the goodness and meaning that underlie her nurturing speak of the reliability and moral order of the world overall. This includes a rudimentary "space/time orientation" (Erikson 1997, 91), as well as what Erikson terms "a convincing pattern of providence" (1964, 116). Of course, mothers' sense of goodness and meaning are distilled from the wider society's "world images" (1997, 91), something that Erikson suggests is exemplified in the Indian notion of *dharma* (1969, 37).

The negative or dystonic quality that opposes the syntonic trust is basic mistrust. The result of the first stage is never purely the positive element, so there is always some factor of mistrust within the infant's psyche, and, in any case, an attitude of total trust would not be well suited to facing life. Erikson sketches mistrust in terms of being

> accompanied by an experience of "total" rage, with fantasies of the total domination or even destruction of the sources of pleasure and provision; and ... such fantasies and rages live on in the individual and are revived in extreme states and situations.
>
> (1968, 82)

The tremendous anger and rage of an infant's or toddler's periodic tantrums really do appear "total," and in this sense it does not seem an exaggeration to speak of the aim as the destruction "of the sources of pleasure and provision," i.e., the meaningful world. Acute mistrust is expressed through "severe estrangement which characterizes individuals who withdraw into themselves when at odds with themselves and with others" (97). Thus, the extent of the dystonic mistrust repeats trust's elements of self, others, world.

Hope is the "virtue" that corresponds to trust, laying the foundation for those qualities that emerge in the later seven psychosocial stages: will, purpose, competence, fidelity, love, care, and wisdom (Erikson 1997, 56–57). The relationship between trust and hope is so intimate that the two are almost synonymous, although trust, perhaps, primarily concerns the present, while the reference to the future is emphasized in Erikson's description of its paired virtue:

> Hope bestows on the anticipated future a sense of leeway inviting expectant leaps, either in preparatory imagination or in small initiating actions. And such daring must count on basic trust in the sense of a trustfulness that must be, literally and figuratively, nourished by maternal care.
>
> (60)

Hope is fostered by trust in the self, others, and world, that there is some justification for one's needs/desires, and that there is some requisite order and meaning in the world such that one can have an expectation of success. In a charming anecdote, Erikson refers to the linguistic tie between hope and hop (60). To take a hop requires trust or confidence in one's abilities, and in a reasonably coherent world—past experience, the laws of nature (gravity), and the stability of basically solid objects (the earth's crust). Still, far beyond this lighthearted example, Erikson's understanding of the crucial role of hope in human life is underscored in two short statements: "Hope connotes the most basic quality of 'I'-ness, without which life could not begin or meaningfully end" (62); and "The shortest formulation of the identity gain of earliest childhood may well be: I am what hope I have and give" (1968, 106–107).

Erikson often concludes his more detailed treatments of basic trust with a discussion of religion, and connects religious faith with both trust and hope—especially mature hope. He speaks of relating "the special strengths emerging from trust and hope with religion" (1997, 82), and of hope as "the ontogenetic basis of faith" (1964, 118). The affiliation with trust in both self and world is unmistakable in his assertion that religious atonement seeks to "restore faith in the goodness of one's strivings and the kindness of the powers of the universe" (1963, 251). In all, hope and faith are so aligned that they forcefully illuminate each other.

While Sigmund Freud elicited the "infantile prototype" in his caustic critique that religion was nothing more than a psychological illusion, Erikson's understanding of the dynamics within the earliest phase of human development actually secured his appreciation for the authentic role of religion in individual and social life. For Freud, such overpowering threats as the powers of nature and death reminded humans of the vulnerability of their childhood and especially their helplessness in the face of the omnipotent father. In response to this later situation of weakness, nature was humanized and it was imagined that through pleading to and petitioning the resultant father-God, nature's powers could be tamed (Freud 1964, 22–26).

Though Erikson did write that "all religions have in common the periodical childlike surrender to a Provider or Providers who dispense earthly fortune as well as spiritual health" (1963, 250), it was for him the mother–infant relationship that revealed the significance of religion in mature human living. While Freud's discourse plays upon the opposition of scientific reality and religious illusion, Erikson's features the interpersonal meaning, order, and goodness associated with trust and hope. He is, as before, particularly interested in the site of the mother–infant face-to-face, writing,

> Here we are again reminded of the lifelong power of the first mutual recognition of the newborn and the *primal* (maternal) *other* and its eventual transfer to the *ultimate other* who will "lift up His countenance upon you and give you peace."
>
> (1997, 88)

Erikson emphasizes the experience and symbolic power of facing a significant other, whether at the beginning of life or anticipating it at the end as the "pervasive quality which we call the *numinous*: the aura of a hallowed presence" (45).

A brief glimpse at Erikson's approach to therapy concludes the discussion of his portrait of trust. The psychoanalytic process is portrayed as a mutual endeavor in which "the two subjectivities join in ... disciplined understanding and shared insight" (1964, 53). Through the "convincing presence of the therapist," patients "dominated by a sense of fragmentation and isolation" can develop an awareness of "wholeness, immediacy and mutuality" (quoted in Schlein 2016, 156). In essence, healing advances through trust in the other.

Trauma

The history of the research and wider interest in trauma is as episodic and fractured as some of the symptoms of the phenomenon itself. The background is the scurrilous pseudo-diagnosis of hysteria, which as the critic M. Micale writes, was "a dramatic medical metaphor for everything that men found mysterious or unmanageable in the opposite sex" (quoted in Herman 2015, 10). The symptoms of this "disorder" included paralysis, sensory loss, convulsions, emotional outbursts, and selective amnesia; the verdict that hysteria was an illness exclusive to women was regarded as incontestable.

Actual research into trauma began with the work on hypnosis and hysteria by the neurologist Jean-Martin Charcot in Paris, starting in the 1860s. His legacy included the careful scientific examination and classification of the symptoms of trauma and the conclusion that it was a psychological disorder that tormented both sexes. Beyond Charcot's famous theatrical demonstrations of some of his patients (Herman 2015, 10), this research drew the serious attention of renowned psychologists including Pierre Janet, William James, and Sigmund Freud. Freud's early work on hysteria and obsessional neurosis as seen in the book *Studies in Hysteria* (1895), authored in collaboration with Joseph Breuer, traced the onset of the disorder to traumatic events. This was particularly the case with their women patients, who after prolonged analysis reported episodes of childhood sexual abuse. However, soon after the publication of this study, Freud abandoned his seduction theory—that "the ultimate cause of hysteria is always the seduction of the child by the adult" (quoted in Van der Kolk 2015, 183)—for his well-known psychosexual model with its emphasis on childhood sexuality and the Oedipal crisis.[5]

In the twentieth century, the topic of trauma only intermittently entered the arenas of scientific journals and public consciousness. Periods of high interest such as World War I and World War II—under the rubrics of shell shock, battle fatigue, and war neurosis—were followed by years of disavowal and inattention. The precious lessons taken from the psychologically disabled soldiers were quickly forgotten—that the disorders were not caused by physiological or mental weakness, but that the terrors of combat were the key, and that recovery depended upon the support of comrades and intensive analytic working-through (the "taking cure") of terrifying memories and feelings, especially shame and self-reproach. Sustained research and retrieval of past breakthroughs only commenced in the 1970s in conjunction with the Vietnam War and the feminist movement. In both cases, it was the victims of trauma who launched the new era. Vietnam veterans suffering from what was later identified as Post-Traumatic Stress Disorder first met together in their own groups, called "rap groups," to discuss past terrors and present, shattered lives. Later, the veterans began to invite psychologists to help in their self-examinations. Women's groups in "consciousness raising sessions" painfully unearthed deeply buried memories of childhood abuse and rape, although their insights were often met with societal indifference or forceful disavowal. In the 1990s and throughout the early twenty-first century these disastrous patterns of reaction were revived as sexual abuse by Catholic priests, and sexual harassment and assault, especially in the workplace (the Me Too movement), again brought the topic of trauma to public attention.

The tortured, partial breakthrough at the scientific level was embodied in the third edition (1980) of *The Diagnostic and Statistical Manual of Mental Disorders* (DSM–III) and the diagnosis of Post-Traumatic Stress Disorder (PTSD). The entry, as summarized by Bessel van der Kolk, is,

A person is exposed to a horrendous event "that involved actual or threatened death or serious injury, or a threat to the physical integrity of self or others," causing "intense fear, helplessness, or horror," which results in a variety of manifestations: intrusive reexperiencing of the event (flashbacks, bad dreams, feeling as if the event were occurring), persistent and crippling avoidance (of people, places, thoughts, or feelings associated with the trauma, sometimes with amnesia for important parts of it), and increased arousal (insomnia, hyper-vigilance, or irritability).

(2015, 158–159)

However, attempts to include a separate diagnosis in later editions of the DSM of "Complex PTSD" for victims of childhood trauma were not successful. Despite this, as the above entry indicates, there are common symptoms for a wide variety of sufferers of PTSD, shared "between rape survivors and combat veterans, between battered women and political prisoners," between survivors of political and domestic "tyrants" (Herman 2015, 3).[6]

Judith Herman

One of the classic texts of continuing relevance is the psychiatrist Judith Herman's *Trauma and Recovery: The Aftermath of Violence—From Domestic Abuse to Political Terror*, first published in 1992, with updates in 1997 and 2015. The book provides an excellent phenomenology of the disorder, organized in two sections on symptoms or more existentially expressed "human adaptation to traumatic events," and recovery (2015, 3). It is particularly germane to the present study in terms of the numerous references to Erikson, especially his notion of basic trust as well as his overall architectonic of psychosocial stages. What is distinctive in her work in terms of the wider literature on trauma is the powerful feminist discussion of the political context that haunts survivors, therapists, and even researchers in the field. The same neglect, evasion, denial, and attack that frequent responses to victims of trauma also attach to those who work or testify on their behalf (1–10).

While there are significant differences in the sources or causes, commencement, duration, and severity of trauma, a distinct "dialectic" pervades the aftermath of the survivor's life. Herman writes that the victim is caught in "opposing psychological states ... between the extremes of amnesia or of reliving the trauma, between floods of intense, overwhelming feeling and arid states of no feeling at all, between irritable, impulsive action and complete inhibition of action" (2015, 47). This oscillation between extremes speaks to a fragmentation or lack of integration that is repeated in the common diagnosis of "dissociation," which is regularly discussed by Herman as well as by other contemporary researchers. Her succinct description of this process is that "intense sensory and emotional experiences are disconnected from the social domain of language and memory" (239). Shards of the traumatic event are held in the mind but are not integrated as are normal experiences. Key sensory and emotional elements are left in pieces, without being contextualized in terms of the typical contours of events, such as place, time, and duration, and earlier and later incidents. From another angle, the narrative structure of both memory and language is missing, which ties together sensations from the outside and subjects' emotional responses in terms of temporality, causation, and the inside/outside and subject/object splits.

More concretely, in the first part of her book, Herman categorizes the symptoms of trauma under the headings of hyperarousal, intrusion, and constriction. Hyperarousal describes an abnormal over-sensitivity to sights and sounds that often elicit fits of severe fear and anger in the subject. Intrusion characterizes a particular kind of helplessness, where sounds and partial scenes overtake the subject throughout the day and night as flashbacks and nightmares. This also involves involuntary reliving of the original horror. Constriction refers to the narrowing of awareness as well as the avoidance of human encounters. The individual lives in a kind of fog of numbness, indifference, detachment, and passivity, sometimes augmented by taking depressants in order to lessen hyperarousal.

Particularly significant, Herman finds that "traumatized people suffer damage to the basic structures of the self" (2015, 56),[7] which includes the sense of oneself, the attitude toward others, and even the approach to life. Emotional attacks turned upon the self, that is, feelings of doubt, shame, and guilt, are pervasive, since victims often unjustifiably attribute painful episodes to some perceived failure on their part. If the traumatic event is perpetrated by known others, either in one's childhood or in later life, the rape, physical or emotional violence, or abuse results in an abiding sense of betrayal. Feelings of distrust toward the whole human community often follow trauma, in part because of the victim's frequent experience of others' refusal to acknowledge what happened or to support their efforts to remember and confront that past. Herman also references Robert Jay Lifton's finding that Vietnam veterans exposed to extreme situations regularly emerged with a sense that the world itself was "counterfeit" (quoted in Herman 2015, 55). Victims were convinced that the human community was totally bereft of any purpose, meaning, or moral foundation. Trauma's impact on the whole structure of meaning in which one lives is well described: "Traumatic events ... undermine the belief systems that give meaning to human experience. They violate the victim's faith in a natural or divine order and cast the victim into a state of existential crisis" (51). Herman quotes a Vietnam veteran who expressed the loss of meaning in the language of faith: "I could not rationalize in my mind how God let good men die" (55).

The second part of Herman's text explores the three phases of recovery: safety, remembrance and mourning, and reconnection. However, almost as a preface to these phases, she introduces the underlying centrality of personal support for the victim, exemplified in the statement, "The single most powerful predictor of therapeutic success is the quality of the relationship between patient and therapist" (2015, 272). Much is required of this latter figure, especially if the traumatic disorder is acute and an overall experience of neglect, evasion, denial, and attack by others has deepened the injury. Establishing an alliance with the victim requires relevant knowledge, experience, and the personal qualities of empathy, sensitivity, and abiding moral support. Even more imposing is the willingness to share the horror, know "terrible things,"[8] face the patient's continual suspicion and rejection, and accept one's own weaknesses, failures, and predilections for violence. The therapist must also acknowledge being responsible for re-traumatizing the victim by having them relive the terrifying event(s) as part of recovery.

Establishing a sense of safety in the patient is the first stage in recovery. The sense of helplessness and vulnerability are universal symptoms of trauma and present early obstacles to recovery. As indicated above, the therapist must painstakingly commence building a sense of personal trust. Attention must be given to the patient's everyday life and wider environment, which involves finances, living arrangements, and the wider social world. These concerns may be especially relevant in cases of domestic violence, rape, and substance abuse. Additionally, the victim must be helped to recover a sense of power over their body. Trauma overwhelms and often incapacities a person; recovering a sense of owning, controlling, and directing one's own body is essential.

The next feature, remembrance, has been highlighted in all of the literature concerning trauma. The flashback and dream fragments of what occurred need to be brought together with what has been forgotten and repressed, the latter often in the service of basic psychological survival. The reconstructed story should recount what has happened, as completely and in depth as possible, in addition to the life before and after the incident(s). This fulsome narrative, the historical framework of time, place, events, and persons, allows the reintegration of the past. However, it is widely agreed that recalled events are not literally replayed in memory.[9] Their reconstruction is influenced by many factors, especially the context of the retelling. Additionally, the story cannot simply be a reiteration of "just the facts." Although a task of extreme difficulty, feelings must be re-experienced and retold with the appropriate affect. To stress this point, Herman quotes Freud and Breuer's early reflection, "Recollection without affect almost invariably produces no result" (Herman 2015, 177).

In this process of expanding on the requisite narrative, Herman enigmatically writes, "the traumatic event challenges an ordinary person to become a theologian, a philosopher, and a jurist" (2015, 178). In constructing their testimony, the survivor is brought to raise almost inevitable questions. That of "Why me?" is unanswerable, but at least improper feelings of self-responsibility, weakness, and guilt can be addressed. In addition, there are "'shattered assumptions' about meaning, order, and justice in the world" (178). Of course, the therapist cannot resolve these issues. Still, according to Herman, they are tasked to "share her own struggles with these intense philosophical questions ... [and] affirm a position of moral solidarity with the survivor" (178). In the process of composing a new narrative or interpretation of the events, the survivor is given the power to voice their own dignity and value. Lastly, telling their story inevitably leads to mourning and grief, which are regarded as the most difficult challenges for remembrance. The mourning for what is lost is especially demanding for those who suffer from childhood abuse or neglect, since the irretrievable loss concerns childhood itself.[10]

"Engagement with life" or reconnection is the final phase in recovery (Herman 2015, 195). Since isolation from others, part of the wider condition of constriction, is a ubiquitous feature of trauma, repair necessitates meeting and joining with others. Relationship with others includes friends and wider groups, which engender sharing experiences, mutual support, and even commitment to universal moral ideals. This latter is important for Herman, because it gives the survivor the power to affirm the significance and reality of justice, even if experience of past evil cannot be erased. In this instance and in terms of confronting trauma overall, recovery is never complete nor repair ever finished, but a life of enjoyment and meaning is possible.

The twin topics of trust and intersubjectivity, paramount in Erikson's *oeuvre*, are also featured in Herman's treatment of trauma. This includes the ways that trauma eviscerates trust, how recovery requires its renewal, and the role of other persons in both processes. The underlying theme that reverberates throughout the discussion of these topics is introduced when Herman cites the definition of trust that Erikson takes from *Webster's Dictionary*: "Trust ... is here [in the dictionary] defined as 'the assured reliance on another's integrity'" (2015, 153).

The issue of trust, its disappearance and recovery, prominently figures in the symptoms of trauma and in the efforts of repair. In brief, hyperarousal, that the individual always feels in danger and that any unexpected sight or sound can lead to paroxysms of fear and anger, clearly represents the loss of trust in everyday life. Constriction, particularly the withdrawal and isolation from others, embodies the failure of trust in the full range of human relationships. Herman explains, "Basic trust ... forms the basis of all systems of relationship," while "traumatic events ... breach the attachments of family, friendship, love, and community" (2015, 51).

Trust is so pertinent to the first stage of recovery, safety, that Herman actually equates the two terms: "the sense of safety in the world, or basic trust ..." (2015, 51). In relation to childhood trauma and the second stage, remembrance and mourning, the author strikingly asserts that the victims "must mourn the loss of the foundation of basic trust, the belief in a good parent" (193). The stage of reconnection is, once again, almost seen as synonymous with trust: "By the third stage of recovery, the survivor has regained some capacity for appropriate trust. She can once again feel trust in others when that trust is warranted" (205). Further, whether Herman is addressing reconnection, "reconciling with oneself" (202), or the dynamics of the "therapeutic relationship," trust is the fundamental issue (138, 205).

Erikson's wider interpersonal or intersubjective perspective on human development and life overall is constantly echoed in *Trauma and Recovery*. For example, in emphasizing the crucial role of relationships in the process of recovery, Herman both surveys Erikson's first few psychosocial stages and includes a footnote to his *Childhood and Society*. She writes,

> In her renewed connections with other people, the survivor re-creates the psychological faculties that were damaged or deformed by the traumatic experience. These faculties include the basic capacities for trust, autonomy, initiative, competence, identity, and intimacy.
>
> (2015, 133)

Herman also repeats Erikson's profound insight concerning the reciprocally enhancing dynamics that pertain to deep human interactions. In what Erikson terms "mutual activation" and she identifies as "a mutually enhancing interaction" (216), which can be found in both interpersonal and group settings,

> when groups develop cohesion and intimacy, a complex mirroring process comes into play. As each participant extends herself to others she becomes more capable of receiving the gifts that others have to offer. The tolerance, compassion and love she grants to others begin to rebound upon herself.
>
> (215–216)

Bessel van der Kolk

The psychiatrist Bessel van der Kolk's *The Body Keeps the Score* (2015) is the "fruit of thirty years of trying to understand how people deal with, survive, and heal from traumatic experiences" (359). The main thrust of the book concerns transformations in the understanding and treatment of trauma by way of new discoveries in neuroscience, developmental psychology, and interpersonal neurobiology. These have produced insights into features of the trauma syndrome which previously were often regarded as either absolutely incredible, or having their origin in the victim's inherent weakness and purposeful deception. The disconnect from the present, and the incursion of fragmented images, sounds, sensations, and emotions from the past, can now be viewed in terms of the ways that the brain processes traumatic information.

The point of departure for the breakthroughs is brain-imaging techniques, which became possible in the early 1990s. Unfortunately, it is at this point that Van der Kolk's use of a much-criticized triune brain model (reptilian, limbic, and rational brain) introduced in the 1960s, compromises some of his presentation.[11] Notwithstanding this problematic, it is clear that traumatic experiences affect dynamic brain systems that receive and process experience. While trauma impacts neural networks, the changes are not necessarily permanent, because the brain is constantly changing as new experiences are recorded and absorbed. This key process is termed neuroplasticity, that is, the flexibility of brain circuits. Various classes of treatments such as pharmacotherapy, physiotherapy, and psychotherapy target different processes or functions of the brain to address the issues of dissociation, hyperarousal, and fragmentation, and to promote the creation of meaningful, narrative memories (Van der Kolk 2015, 55–58).

Developmental psychology, or its new branch of developmental psychopathology—"the study of the impact of adverse experiences on the development of mind and brain" (Van der Kolk 2015, 2)—is a second principal focus of *The Body Keeps the Score*. This is justified by Van der Kolk's contention that developmental trauma is "The Hidden Epidemic" (151), that is, childhood neglect and violence underlie such seemingly indomitable societal phenomena as poverty, homelessness, incarceration rates, and substance abuse. As discussed above, the early interactions between mother and child provide the template or "inner map" for safety, danger, trust, self-care, agency, and how the self, others, and the world are perceived (131). Neuroscience explores some of the processes behind the intense attachment and attunement in infancy and early childhood.

Recognition of the centrality of the interpersonal in development and the perennial human quest for meaning have had an increasing impact on the understanding and treatment of trauma. Interspersed throughout Van der Kolk's text are such sentiments as,

> Social support is the most powerful protection against becoming overwhelmed by stress and trauma. ... The critical issue is *reciprocity*: being truly heard and seen by the people around us, feeling that we are held in someone else's mind and heart.
>
> (2015, 81)

> The role of those relationships [with family, loved ones, community] is to provide physical and emotional safety, including safety from feeling shamed, admonished, or judged, and to bolster the courage to tolerate, face, and process the reality of what has happened.
>
> (212)

One deeply intriguing and illuminating example of a treatment for developmental trauma draws upon this essential social dimension of human life. Given the extreme importance of the interactions within the mother–infant dyad, it is not surprising that persons who suffered from early neglect or abuse face the most intractable hurdles for recovery. How can treatments utilize initial experiences of care and trust when these are wanting? Van der Kolk describes the formation of "virtual memories" through a kind of psychomotor therapy or theatre, with real persons in a therapy group replacing an individual's early family members, and providing the missing warmth, care, and encouragement (306–310). The success of such imaginative tableaux testifies to the protean character of memory and the neuroplasticity of the brain.

Three psychoanalysts

Robert D. Stolorow's *Trauma and Human Existence: Autobiographical, Psychoanalytic and Philosophical Reflections* (2007) reinforces many of the themes of the prior two examinations as well as extending some lines of inquiry. It amplifies the significance of intersubjectivity in lived human existence and in the devastating phenomenon of trauma, pursuing these through the lens of emotional life. Emotions and feelings, or affect, are not seen as spontaneous eruptions inside the isolated individual, but as arising within the context of relationships between persons.

For Stolorow, as well as the other psychologists discussed here, the earliest engagements between the infant/child and the primary caregiver(s) are a crucial focus. As we have seen, myriad features of the foundational sense of self and others, as well as the approach to the world, emerge out of this dynamic. The infant's original "inchoate, diffuse, and largely bodily experiences" are crystallized, named, and integrated into wider temporal and narrative perspectives through the caregiver's "attuned responsiveness" to the subject's developing needs (2007, 29). Such responses include subtle bodily and vocal initiatives and reactions, as well as the later full use of language.

Developmental trauma is the result of abuse, neglect, or the lack of appropriate attunement by the caregiver to frightening feelings or "developmental yearnings" (Stolorow 2007, 4) of the infant or child. This is the backdrop for Stolorow's decisive words, *"Pain is not pathology"* (10). It is the overall response or interpersonal context which makes emotional pain unbearable. In traumatic situations the child must first of all maintain the semblance of a relationship, and then deal with the misaligned feelings. The latter is done through dissociation, taking up the perspective of the emotionally absent or abusive parent, blaming themselves for the situation, and finally, overlaying the experience with feelings of shame and badness (10).

The fundamental dynamics that underlie childhood trauma also appertain to traumatic episodes that appear later in life, that is, both are intersubjective affairs. For Stolorow, the intensity and even presence of trauma in response to an event is contingent on "the extent to which there is someone available who can provide a relational home wherein the [traumatic] anxiety can be held, understood, articulated, and integrated" (2007, 33–34). Put another way, what ultimately is experienced by the individual as traumatic is determined by "whatever feels unacceptable, intolerable, or too dangerous in particular intersubjective contexts" (4). Consequently, in addition to the investigation and articulation of the prior traumatic situation, successful therapy requires the analyst's ability to supply the missing environment of receptivity and understanding.[12]

Stolorow elevates the lessons of trauma to the degree that they are "a fundamental constituent of our existential constitution" (2007, 48). This conclusion revolves around what he considers the "absolutisms of everyday life" (13). Often following the philosopher Martin Heidegger, Stolorow portrays human life as precarious and vulnerable, and human relationships as, obviously, finite. Through relationships with others, humans build various canopies of trust and meaning, that is, "naive realism and optimism that allow one to function in the world, experienced as stable and predictable" (16). In Stolorow's view, trauma fundamentally rips these apart, revealing their quality as façade, a veneer covering impending finitude. Human relationships are the precarious islands of safety within this portrait, but they ultimately must give way to the darkness (50).

Donna Orange's presentation of a "hermeneutics of trust" (2011, 31–35) in *The Suffering Stranger* also highlights some of the insights detailed above, developed in conjunction with conceptions from psychoanalysts such as Erik Erikson, Sándor Ferenczi, and D. W. Winnicott, and the philosophers Emmanuel Levinas, Paul Ricoeur, and Hans-Georg Gadamer. Her asymmetrical approach of trust and welcoming toward the one who suffers stands in contrast to the more customary psychoanalytic attitude, a hermeneutics of suspicion, that seeks to unearth the "true" meaning behind the patient's words, dreams, defense, and resistance. Defense and resistance are not seen by Orange as acts of hostility, but as earlier constructed symptoms of trying to live with, rather than being destroyed by, trauma. She defines her approach: "Above all, we trust the other to teach us. As psychoanalysts, we rely on the patient to teach us about her or his suffering, we search for meaning—both found and created—together" (206). Following from this, the analyst's empathy, understanding, and trust, much as in the model of the attuned mother's response to her child, are what create the patient's trust in self, others, and world. In the end, Orange's stance assumes a common world in which dignity is to be restored to the "devastated, shame-filled, degraded, and suffering human beings like ourselves" (71).

Jessica Benjamin's approach to collective and individual trauma presented in Chapter 1 foreshadows many themes explored in this chapter, but particularly valuable and supplementary to the present examination are her discussions of the challenges that arise in addressing both types of trauma. In exploring the schism between the passive bystander to collective trauma and the authentic witness, as well as the conflicting psychological forces within both victims and perpetrators, Benjamin focuses on two countervailing processes, splitting and identification. Splitting distances and denigrates those who suffer by separating "us" from "them," "doer" from "done-to," the safe, successful, and chosen from the exposed, and ultimately the dignified from the discarded. Identification and empathy with the oppressed, which are the hallmarks of witnessing, dignify the victim and establish a path toward healing.

Among the challenges that Benjamin explores in the clinical treatment of individual trauma is the victim's sense of their own guilt, of their experience isolating them from others, and of their fear that the world itself is manifestly counterfeit and unjust. As a psychotherapist Benjamin finds that she is tasked with conveying some fundamental principles, which cannot just be pieces of information communicated to the patient. Healing requires that Benjamin testify in her person, through actions—knowing terrible things, witnessing devastating injury, acknowledging injustice, and together, working-through repair.

In response to these compelling collective and individual situations, Benjamin formulates the ideal of the moral third, "of the moral power that acknowledges and affirms what is lawful, what is wrong, what should never happen to a child, to a human being" (2018, 213). The moral third comprises the fundamental trust in: the inherent dignity of all persons, the connection to and responsibility for others, and a transcendent lawfulness or "larger principle of necessity, rightness, goodness" (2007, 9).

Preliminary lessons

There are many correlations, in the peculiar sense of negative correspondences, between the phenomena of trust and trauma. This is particularly the case when exploring features of the trauma syndrome. Overall, trust emphasizes integration and connection, while trauma features fragmentation and alienation. Consequently, surveying either side of this dialectic illuminates essential elements of the other side. Examination of the processes of recovery from trauma is equally valuable because trust constitutes its indispensable beginning, means, and goal.

Herman's equating basic trust with safety (2015, 51), and perhaps a sense of comfort, stability, support, and hope, provides one approach to these dynamic relationships. The DSM–III characterizes the symptoms of trauma as "intense fear, helplessness, or horror," which stand at the opposite side of trust/safety. Establishing a sense of safety in the patient is always the first, unconditional requirement in the process of recovery, and the eventual goal is to feel safe (trusting) enough in the world to go forward with life. Both safety and trust underlie what Stolorow describes as the "absolutisms of everyday life" that "allow one to function in the world, experienced as stable and predictable"[13] (2007, 16).

The three primary dimensions of both trust and trauma are the same: the self, others, and the world (Erikson 1968, 96). A trust in one's own body (1963, 248), a sense of one's overall goodness and "trustworthiness" (1968, 96), and a personal feeling of unity and consistency are some of the significant achievements in Erikson's portrayal of the first psychosocial stage. Alternatively, trauma is regularly described by, and recovery must consistently address, a lack of sensitivity to and understanding of one's body and a pervasive sense of vulnerability, doubt, shame, and guilt. The infant's trust in others begins with that preeminent other who shows consistent love and care. Trauma is always accompanied by a distrust of and alienation from the whole human community, which frequently develops from the victim's experiences of indifference, rejection, and even attack by loved ones, friends, and acquaintances. The idea that trust is related to an understanding of the world is expressed in a number of ways by Erikson. He speaks of "basic trust ... in mere existence" (1963, 249), which includes a sense of goodness or moral order that the mother draws from the wider society. Examples of world order include "a pattern of providence" (1964, 116), and the Indian notion of *dharma*, "a consolidation of the world through the self-realization of each individual within a joint order" (1969, 37). Trauma ruptures this portrait of a meaningful world. The world is now experienced as "counterfeit" (Herman 2015, 57), with no just or moral core; consequently, recovery requires the "ordinary person to become a theologian, a philosopher, and a jurist" (178).

The underlying feature of the interpersonal or intersubjective permeates every investigation of trust and trauma. As cited earlier, Erikson's equivalence of trust and the support of the other is underscored by his reference to trust as "the assured reliance on another's integrity" (1963, 269). This begins, obviously, in infancy:

> Our interactions with our caregivers convey what is safe and what is dangerous: whom we can count on and who will let us down; what we need to do to get our needs met ... [all of this] forms the template of how we think of ourselves and the world around us.
>
> (Van der Kolk 2015, 131)

Recovery is clearly about the understanding and encouragement of others, with Van der Kolk asserting, "The critical issue is *reciprocity*: being truly heard and seen by the people around us, feeling that we are held in someone else's mind and heart" (81). This is even more applicable to the interaction in therapy, as Herman writes: "The single most powerful predictor of therapeutic success is the quality of the relationship between patient and therapist" (2015, 272). Further, the therapist must rely on the support of colleagues and friends, for *"no one can face trauma alone"* (153). The deeply intersubjective perspective is also provided by Stolorow, who sees the presence or absence of personal support for the victim as decisive in the very pathology of trauma,[14] especially in the case of developmental trauma. Trauma arises when "severe emotional pain cannot find a relational home" (2007, 10).

The dialectical opposition between trust and trauma arises in conjunction with several other themes, including hope, meaning, and narrative. Hope is the first psychosocial virtue or accomplishment in Erikson's portrayal: "The shortest formulation of the identity gain of earliest childhood may well be: I am what hope I have and give" (1968, 106–107). The anguish, estrangement, and helplessness of victims of trauma means that hope is also one of the first casualties, and fittingly, a major task of treatment is "to cope with the hopelessness of ... patients" (quoted in Herman 2015, 144).

The term "meaning" appears in many places in the psychological literature; while usually not explicitly defined, its use implies something that arises from fulfilling relationships and has a place within a wider, valuable context.[15] The idea that meaning has an intersubjective dimension is reflected in Erikson's assertion that parents "must also be able to represent to the child a deep, an almost somatic conviction that there is a meaning to what they are doing" (1963, 249), and Van der Kolk's view that "safe connections ['being able to feel safe with other people'] are fundamental to meaningful and satisfying lives" (2015, 81). Some of the content of this meaning is provided through Benjamin's concept of the moral third. The moral third refers to a trust in a transcendent lawfulness or moral dimension, "a larger principle of necessity, rightness, goodness" (2007, 9). Seen in this way, the topic of meaning can also be examined, as it is above, in relation to that third object of basic trust, the world. The absence of meaning that is palpable to the trauma sufferer is presented by Herman in terms of the "'shattered assumptions' about meaning, order, and justice in the world" (2015, 178).

The topic of narrative, in the sense of individuals being able to recall and narrate events in the context of their own life history, is one of the perennial topics within the literature about the treatment of trauma. Briefly, looking at the present discussion, Erikson believes that success within the first psychosocial stage includes the ability to see experience within a rudimentary "space-time orientation" (1997, 91). Herman's paradigmatic presentation of the second stage of recovery focuses on the nature of the requisite trauma story: "Out of the fragmented components of frozen imagery and sensation, patient and therapist slowly reassemble an organized, detailed, verbal account, oriented in time and historical context" (2015, 177).

The examination of trauma has added new perspectives to the notion of basic trust, in the sense that the extent and devastating power of trauma provides a mirror image of the compass and strength of trust. The question arises whether a new approach is also available to the issue of trust's dynamic antithesis, which for Erikson is mistrust. He holds that some mistrust in life is necessary, and envisions trust and mistrust in a relationship of uneven "balance" (1968, 325). In addition, he explains that "mistrust can contaminate all aspects of our lives and deprive us of love and fellowship with human beings" (1997, 107).[16] However, if the earlier portrayal of trauma is relevant here, mistrust, even acute mistrust, is not a strong enough term to either characterize the terror, vulnerability, and fragmentation of trauma or to stand as trust's full polar opposite. Turning to the "virtue" of hope, which corresponds to trust, can be helpful. In the French language the opposite pole of hope/*espoir* is despair/*desespoir*. The power of the term despair is entirely adequate to the hopelessness, as well as the other features endemic to the trauma syndrome, such as feelings of fear, terror, and helplessness; alienation from others; and seeing the world as inalterably corrupt. Despair is also fully satisfactory to portray the overall condition in which the victim of trauma finds themself, haunted by the sense that one's life, at whatever stage, just cannot go on.[17] In all, is perhaps despair, rather than mistrust, a more appropriate dystonic partner throughout life's stages to that foundational notion of basic trust?[18]

Finally, it is important to note that there is a fundamental synergy among what Erikson terms "basic trust" and crucial conceptions in the works of many of the clinical theorists examined in this chapter: the notion of safety in Herman and Van der Kolk's treatments, Stolorow's "absolutisms of everyday life," and Benjamin's lynchpin "moral third."[19] Herman equates basic trust with the "sense of safety in the world" (2015, 51), and, consequently, finds that in response to trauma's devastation, the "central task of the first stage [of recovery] is the establishment of safety" (155). For Van der Kolk, "physical and emotional safety" is central to both trusting in the self and facing the tests of the wider world (2015, 212).

Stolorow sees these "absolutized horizons of normal everydayness" as "the basis for a kind of naïve [sic] realism and optimism that allow one to function in the world, experienced as stable and predictable" (2007, 16). Further information about this normally taken for granted horizon is unearthed by Stolorow's description of the effects of emotional trauma where a "deep chasm [appears] in which an anguished sense of estrangement and solitude takes form" (16). Trust's underlying elements of feeling connected to responsive others, the world as ordered and meaningful, and a basic optimism about life itself can be glimpsed beneath Stolorow's two-fold account.

While Benjamin's view of the moral third features a number of trust's components in relation to the self, others, and the world, it is particularly the ethical and transcendent quality of life that is emphasized. As noted just above, the moral third comprises the trust in, belief in, faith in the intrinsic value of all persons, the essential interdependence of the human community, and a transcendent moral order. In contrast, Benjamin sees trauma precipitating "the feeling of a broken or fragmented self, ... a vision of the world as collapsed, ruined or broken. ... Its sense or meaning is precarious" (2018, 87).

All four concepts—"basic trust," "safety," "the absolutisms of everyday life," "the moral third,"—are seen as emerging out of the relationship between mother and infant, and continue their relevance throughout life. Or, transposing an element from Erikson's portrayal of hope, these four provide complementary insights into that "without which life could not begin or meaningfully end" (1997, 62).

Notes

1 Joan M. Erikson writes of a ninth stage—"Despair and Disgust vs. Integrity: Wisdom"—at the end of the extended version of *The Life Cycle Completed* (Erikson 1997, 105–114).
2 Stephen Schlein discusses what he terms Erikson's "interpersonal-relational perspective" in his work (2016, 7).

3 The issue of whether care for the self or self-love has an intersubjective origin is latent within a number of the approaches to trust and trauma. Discussions of treatment often imply that beneath the pathological experience, even if it occurs in early childhood, there is a natural love of self which can be called upon and nurtured. Van der Kolk's presentation is more explicit than usual and, thus, quite illustrative:

> Beneath the surface of the protective parts [adaptations] of the trauma survivors there exists an undamaged essence, a Self that is confident, curious, calm, a Self that has been sheltered from destruction. … The Self will spontaneously emerge, and … can be enlisted in the healing process.
>
> (2015, 285)

> For Joan to be able to deal with her misery and hurt, we would have to recruit her own strength and self-love, enabling her to heal herself.
>
> (289)

In contrast to this perspective, Erikson provides a more interpersonal view of the genesis of the self as well as self-love. For him, as we have seen, it is within the mother–infant dyad that the child's understanding of themselves as distinct, and trust in themselves and their own goodness, are developed (1964, 120); and, the "primal other … also becomes the guarantor of a kind of self love … and thus provides that *basic trust*" (1997, 49).

4 Hans Loewald writes of the "mother–infant matrix" which provides the enduring foundation for mental life and behavior, and constitutes the infant's world (1978, 37).

5 Much has been written about this controversial *virage*; see for example Herman 2015, 13–15.

6 Still, there may be important differences in the experience and embodiment of trauma in terms of gender, ethnicity, socio-economic status, and other markers. Commenting on an article by Jill Salberg, Susannah Heschel highlights some intriguing issues regarding trauma, gender, and community. In this case it concerns how women within the Jewish community, because they traditionally represent weakness and vulnerability, might have become "the bearers of [Holocaust] trauma legacies within the family or even the wider Jewish community" (2016, 182). Put in another way, it is a question of "how women experience and somaticize trauma in the context of a religious community whose power and authority lies in the hands of men" (182).

7 Peter Vermeulen's "The Biopolitics of Trauma," in *The Future of Trauma Theory*, offers an important critique of the "Eurocentricism" he sees in the prevailing notion of the self within the literature on trauma. This is part of the wider social and cultural purview that some recent studies of trauma have taken up. He writes,

> Trauma studies have long been dominated by the idea—which can be traced back to the psychoanalytic tradition that informed this field—that trauma is essentially a sudden and punctual event that afflicts the subject from without. This notion all too easily assumes a solid and stable sense of self that is simply not available to many disenfranchised groups, and thus fails to account for the detrimental effects of the "ongoing and sustained dynamics of social injury and deprivation" that affect the lives of non-dominant groups suffering from social injuries such as "racism, misogyny, homophobia, and economic exploitation."
>
> (2014, 144)

8 Martha Bragin describes the therapist's challenge of knowing terrible things:

> The clinician attempting to treat such patients ["survivors of extreme violence"] may be placed in a dilemma: how to convey the capacity to know terrible things without being destroyed by the survivor, while at the same time not conveying that one is dangerous oneself.
>
> (2007, 229)

9 Richard McNally writes, "Recollection is always reconstruction ... The living brain is dynamic and even the most vivid traumatic memories are not literal, unchanging reproductions of what occurred" (2005, 818).

10 Childhood neglect or abuse is the most difficult type of trauma to treat, in large extent because little basic trust was ever established. The process of recovery, which includes connecting to or reinvigorating the trust that was earlier founded, is haunted by this absence. Still, in these extreme cases, the efforts to install trust are perhaps the most revealing.

11 There are a number of critiques of the triune brain model or theory, including in terms of nervous system evolution (Cesario, Johnson, and Eisthen 2020) and brain connectivity (Sporns 2007).

12 The significance of the response of others to the child's traumatic experience was fully understood by Ferenczi. He writes that "the lasting effect of the trauma stems from the absence of a kind, understanding, and enlightening environment" (1988, 210), and "the presence of someone with whom one can share and communicate joy and sorrow (love and understanding) can HEAL the trauma" (201).

13 I have dispensed with the first word in this quotation, "naïve." Living fully in the world through trust is only "naïve" from some perspectives.

14 A similar view of the significance of the intersubjective context in the genesis of trauma is brought to light in Nouri Gana's "Trauma Ties: Chiasmus and Community in Lebanese Civil War Literature." She refers to Paul Shabad, who "explains how unwitnessed solitary suffering transforms into trauma and how only 'the transformation of experienced suffering into witnessed reality at the moment it occurs inoculates experience against traumatization'" (Gana 2014, 86).

15 See the author's chapter "Revisiting an 'Illusion': On Meaning" in *Contemporary Psychoanalysis and Modern Jewish Philosophy* (Oppenheim 2017, 135–167).

16 This statement is from the extended part of the book *The Life Cycle Completed* (Erikson 1997). It is not clear whether this part of the section is authored by Joan M. Erikson or includes material from her husband.

17 Despair is also Søren Kierkegaard's (Anti-Climacus) psychological "sickness unto death," standing as the "opposite" to faith (trust) in that ultimate supporting Other (1980, 49).

18 Erik Erikson's all-encompassing eighth stage is ego integrity vs. despair, but it seems to me that despair, like trust, also underlies all the earlier stages.

19 While Orange's compelling account of the "hermeneutics of trust" is essentially a description of her clinical approach to traumatic suffering, it supplements this discussion of basic trust and its psychoanalytic equivalents.

3 Not "Any Tom, Dick, and Harry"

Abraham Joshua Heschel and Martin Buber confront the Holocaust

In the midst of Abraham Joshua Heschel's most fervent and enigmatic book, *A Passion for Truth* (1974), there is a brief reference to Martin Buber. Heschel writes,

> Martin Buber's declaration "Nothing can make me believe in a God who punishes Saul because he did not murder his enemy" must be contrasted with the Kotzker's statement "A God whom any Tom, Dick and Harry could comprehend, I would not believe in."
>
> (292–293)

Although Heschel merely juxtaposes Buber's view to that of the Kotzker rabbi, Rabbi Menachem Mendel of Kotzk (1787–1859), there is no doubt that this constitutes a stinging rebuke. Is this judgment fair? Is there really so much distance between himself and Buber in terms of understanding God's actions in history?

A Passion for Truth is recognized as both an extremely significant and uncharacteristic book by scholars, as well as by Heschel himself. He produced an immense authorship, starting with his doctoral dissertation on prophetic consciousness, and including such well-known philosophic works in English as *Man is Not Alone* and *God in Search of Man*. There is also a large group of Yiddish writings, which range from topical articles to later published writings on Hasidism. What characterizes the overall *oeuvre* is precisely the affirmation that humans are "not alone." Although God's presence is not always easily discovered, it can be found in many places, including the words of the Prophets, the commandments of Jewish Law (*Halakhah*), and even in the sublimity of nature. In this connection, Heschel saw his task as transforming the indifferent into true seekers, progressively attuning them to the questions God addresses to His deeply loved creatures. This "depth theology" knows of evil, true struggle, of waiting and even anguish, but the overriding tone is one of optimism.

But what of this last book, lying on his desk at his death and posthumously published? The introduction provides Heschel's own reflections on the nature of this writing. He acknowledges his lifelong, passionate connection to Hasidism, especially to the tradition of its founder, Israel ben Eliezer, the *Baal Shem Tov* (Master of the Good Name, d. 1760), "the Besht." Few have been able to convey the joy that launched this latest expression of Jewish mysticism as well as Heschel. He recognized his own spirit in that of the Besht. Both sought to overcome evil through *mitzvoth* (God's commandments), suffering through joy, and absence through prayer. Yet, the book is not just a panegyric to the Besht, but a dialogue between him and his oftentimes reluctant follower, the Kotzker. For Heschel, the latter stood in almost diametric opposition to his master, skeptical that human lies were burying truth, human weakness was conquering strength, and superficiality emerging victorious over depth.

In a few words, Heschel seems to allude to what might have finally brought him to a haunting doubt that his own lifelong choice for the Besht over the Kotzker might have been wrong: "Life in our time has been a nightmare for many of us, tranquility an interlude, happiness a fake. Who could breathe at a time when man was engaged in murdering the holy witness to God six million times?" (1974, 300–301).

The section "A Barrel Full of Holes" of *A Passion for Truth*, which contains Heschel's allusion to Buber, directly addresses the philosophical or theological[1] challenges of the Holocaust. In coming to an assessment of the meaning and validity of Heschel's reference, the wider context of both of their confrontations with that event will be required.[2] Consequently, our discussion will consist of a number of steps: brief biographies of these two modern Jewish philosophers; a review of their most important writings on the Holocaust; a critical examination of three major issues raised in the secondary literature; and an analysis and final commentary on Heschel's critique. We will come to see that Heschel's assessment was both correct and incorrect. Towards the end of their lives, both Jewish philosophers were brought to revolutionary, that is, personally unanticipated and unwanted, conclusions in their struggle with that "*Tremendum*," which is the Holocaust.[3]

Abraham Joshua Heschel was born in Warsaw, Poland in 1907 and died in 1972 in New York City. He had prominent Hasidic lineages on both sides of his family, and received an impressive traditional Jewish education during his early years. Although quickly recognized as a prodigy, he went to Germany to study modern philosophy and eventually received his doctorate. Heschel taught at the Frankfurt *Lehrhaus*, founded by the Jewish philosopher Franz Rosenzweig, and then became its director in 1937. Following *Kristallnacht*, the Nazi pogrom of November 9–10, 1938, he was deported to Warsaw. Just before the German invasion of Poland in 1939, he escaped to London and then continued to the United States in 1940. Heschel later wrote of his brush with the Holocaust,

> My destination was New York, it would have been Auschwitz or Treblinka. I am a brand plucked from the fire, in which my people was burned to death ... [on] an altar of Satan on which millions of human lives were exterminated to evil's greater glory.
>
> (2009, 3)

Despite Heschel's efforts to save his immediate family, he lost almost all of them and a countless number of relatives in the Holocaust. In America Heschel became a prominent Jewish writer and also civil rights activist. He taught at Hebrew Union College in Cincinnati and later at New York's Jewish Theological Seminary.

Martin Buber was born in Vienna, Austria, in 1878 and died in Jerusalem in 1965. His advanced studies were in Germany, where he wrote a dissertation on "individuation" in the thought of the great medieval Christian mystics Meister Eckhart and Jacob Boehme. Buber was a well-known and influential European intellectual by the first decade of the twentieth century. His early books placed him clearly as a spokesman for the Neo-Romantic movement. Adherents of this youth movement rebelled against what they saw as the stifling and alienating modern bourgeois culture and values of their fathers' generation. They countered this with interests in aesthetic and mystic experience and a search for "true community." By 1923, with the publication of *I and Thou*, Buber had replaced this emphasis on aesthetic and mystic experience with the recognition of the consummate powers of dialogue.[4] Buber taught at the University of Frankfurt as well as Rosenzweig's *Lehrhaus*, which he directed from 1933 to 1937. He was an important figure in the emerging Zionist movement, and continued his involvement as a powerful thinker and critic throughout his life. A leader of the Jewish community in Germany from the rise of Nazism in 1933, he left for Palestine in 1938. In Palestine, and later Israel, he was known and respected as a teacher, writer, and philosopher at the Hebrew University in Jerusalem, as well as a ceaseless worker for the cause of Israeli–Arab rapprochement.

There were important interactions between Buber and Heschel before each was forced out of Germany. Of note in the present context was an exchange of letters in 1935, commencing at the initiative of the younger and relatively unknown Heschel (Kaplan and Dresner 1998, 219–228). The correspondence foreshadowed continuing differences in their thought, but is also remarkable in that their critiques of each other showed an interesting parallel. The point of departure was Heschel's dissertation on the biblical Prophets, which he suspected Buber had unfavorably reviewed for a publisher a few years earlier. On his part, Heschel was critical of Buber's I–Thou philosophy in its application to the relationship to God. Heschel felt that the notion of dialogue gave too much prominence to the human side of that relationship, and thus could open the way for a humanist narrative that could jettison the divine from religious life. Buber, in turn, was suspicious of Heschel's emphasis on human access to the inner life of God in his portrayal of the Prophets. He saw this as possibly being explained as a purely human projection, which would then have the result of the divine partner disappearing. There was also a deep division between Heschel and Buber in terms of the legitimacy of *Halakhah* as a means for contact with God. Heschel believed that God gave the gift of *Halakhah* to the Jewish people as a passionate expression of his love. For Buber, *Halakhah* was just the human response to a divine–human encounter that was essentially ineffable.

Selected writings on the Holocaust

Heschel and Buber addressed the philosophical questions of divine providence and theodicy raised by the Holocaust in a number their works. The following is a brief overview of these discussions, consisting of a précis of four treatments by each of them. In Heschel's first important work in the English language, *Man is Not Alone* (1951), the chapter "The Hiding of God" addresses God's relationship to the Holocaust. It begins with a question: "For us, contemporaries and survivors of history's most terrible horrors, it is impossible to meditate about the compassion of God without asking: Where is God?" (151). Heschel's answer is explicit. The Holocaust does not pose a problem for God, since it essentially concerns human actions and human responsibility. It is they who have turned from and thus silenced God, rather than God himself being silent. Heschel uses biblical and liturgical references to impress this point. He both legitimates expressions of anguish and reaffirms ultimate faith in God by ending this section with the whole 26 verses of *Psalm 44*, which concludes, "For our soul is bowed down to the dust; our belly cleaveth unto the earth. Arise for our help, and redeem us for Thy mercies sake" (157).

God in Search of Man (1955), the second of Heschel's signature philosophical works, refers to the Holocaust in a late chapter, "The Problem of Evil." He writes,

> This essential predicament of man [our disturbing familiarity with human evil] has assumed a peculiar urgency in our time, living as we do in a civilization where factories were established in order to exterminate millions of men, women, and children.
>
> (369)

Heschel's response is that through the commandments we can begin to redeem the world, which also awaits God's messianic redemption.

Heavenly Torah: As Refracted through the Generations (Heschel 2007) was originally published in Hebrew in three volumes as *Torah Min ha-Shamayim* of 1962.[5] In the first volume, Heschel includes a discussion of the competing views concerning God's relationship to evil and suffering offered by the two preeminent second century authorities, Rabbi Ishmael and Rabbi Akiva. He uses Akiva, who was martyred by the Romans during the Bar Kokhba revolt, to put forward his own position, with an eye on the Holocaust.[6] According to Heschel's portrayal, Ishmael has a consistent rationalistic outlook on the relationship to God that still recognizes the limitations of human reason. He sees suffering as punishment for human sin, and protests to God when this equation does not seem to be in evidence. Akiva has a more intimate understanding of the relationship to

God. Not only does God suffer along with humans, but in some cases the suffering of innocents can be seen as a paradoxical gift, that is, as a means to deepen their intimate love of God. Accordingly, Heschel writes,

> the greatness of afflictions [suffering] is not only because they cleanse a person's sins, but because within them there is human participation in the afflictions of heaven. No one truly understands the meaning of love, nor does one even know whether he is in love, except through affliction.

> (135)

In reference to the Holocaust, Heschel's treatment places the responsibility for evil fully on humans and is an affirmation of God's ultimate justice.

A Passion for Truth (1974) is somewhat analogous to Heschel's two-volume Yiddish work *Kotsk: The Struggle for Truth* of 1973. As in earlier books, a particular chapter, "The Kotzker and Job," addresses poignant questions about evil and suffering, with some reference to the Holocaust. This background is made unmistakable by the statement quoted above: "Life in our time has been a nightmare for many of us, tranquility an interlude, happiness a fake. Who could breathe at a time when man has engaged in murdering the holy witness to God six million times?" (300–301). A key section in this chapter offers a story to encapsulate the challenges that the Holocaust poses to the life of faith. "Barrels Full of Holes" relates a story from the midrashic literature told by the Kotzker to some of his followers. In it, a king hires laborers to fill barrels that are punctured with holes. One of the workers complains about the futility of this exercise, in seeing the water just trickle out. However, a wise worker replies, "Surely I am to be paid for every barrel! I shall fill them; for this clearly means that my obedience is important to the king" (286).

The level of intensity, actually what many characterize as anguish, of this chapter is unmatched even in an authorship known for its passion. Heschel intersperses challenges with responses in a continuing spiral of emotion. The key question is about the apparent meaninglessness or even absurdity of human existence. He struggles with myriad answers, many of which he has offered before: the task is to obey God; there is meaning beyond absurdity; it is humans who are responsible for injustice; perhaps what is intended is that the barrels be repaired; there will ultimately be compensation for the toil; to stand before the grandeur of the universe and declare it all absurd is "idiotic"; our defining task is to search for truth; we can still carry out some meaningful pursuits; God shares in our suffering; and faith is "compassion for God." It is in this context that Heschel refers to Buber's criticism of the biblical story about God punishing Saul for not killing the Amalekite king. Heschel's indictment is clear: What right does Buber have to limit God to his own understanding of justice? However, it is not evident that Heschel is satisfied with any of the answers. In an earlier section he uses the Kotzker to once again raise his own query, one that haunts the text: "the thought that ultimately God Himself was responsible for the inherent falsehood of human existence" (1974, 233).[7]

The sites that mark Buber's most significant reflections on the Holocaust are more diverse than the references in book chapters we noted in the Heschel *oeuvre*. The essay "Dialogue between Heaven and Earth" (1967b, 214–225) was first given as a French lecture in 1950. The background motif of the essay is performed by its title, that the teaching of the Bible is that "our life is a dialogue between the above and the below" (215). However, according to Buber, the Bible also knows of times when God's providence seems to have disappeared. He supports this statement with a quotation from the prophet Isaiah (8:17), who speaks of a time when God "hideth His face from the house of Jacob" (222). Building upon this, Buber refers again to Isaiah who describes such times as "barbarous," and to Job (30:21) who even speaks of the "cruel God." Of course, God's response to Job is well known; no apology or explanation is forthcoming for this righteous man's suffering. Rather, God only appears and is heard once more. In one of the most startling and powerful statements in Buber's huge literature, he concludes that what is left in such times, our time, is to struggle for justice, contest God's silence, and await His enigmatic presence:

> No, rather even now we contend, we too, with God, even with Him, the Lord of Being, whom we once, we here, chose for our Lord. We do not put up with earthly being; we struggle for its redemption, and struggling we appeal to the help of our Lord, who is again and still a hiding one. In such a state we await His voice, whether it comes out of the storm or out of a stillness that follows it. Though His coming appearance resemble no earlier one, we shall recognize again our cruel and merciful Lord.
>
> (225)

The next document is a letter Buber wrote in 1950 to an acquaintance, Ernsz Szilagyi (2003a, 172–173). The letter supplements the advice of the above essay, about living in a time of God's absence. Buber poses three choices in this situation: to just withdraw from the world (perhaps having in mind his early work on world-renouncers in Hinduism and Buddhism), to admit that the world has no meaning, or to accept *in faith* that God is just. Answering his own question, "How is Jewish life after Auschwitz possible?" he writes,

> Today I no longer know exactly what Jewish life is, and I am not sure it will be known to me in the future. But I know what it means to cling to Him. The ones who continue to cling to Him are pointing toward what could justly be called in the future Jewish life.
>
> (173)

"God and the Spirit of Man" (Buber 1952, 123–129) was a lecture of 1951 delivered in the United States and later published as a chapter in the book

Eclipse of God. While the Holocaust does not enter as a subject, the text adds an important strand to the wider fabric of Buber's reflections on what has happened to the relationship to God. He carefully describes the ways that philosophers and religious persons have succeeded in the effort to silence God. The former have made God a mere object of reflection. The latter have sought to manipulate him according to their wishes and designs. In all, the damage done to the relationship to God is caused by the apotheosis of the human subject, the "I." In his words,

> In our age the I-It [the self-absorbed and objectifying] relation, gigantically swollen, has usurped, practically uncontested, the mastery and the rule. The I of this relation, an I that possesses all, makes all, succeeds with all, this I that is unable to say Thou, unable to meet a being essentially, is the lord of the hour.
>
> (129)

Lastly, as part of a group of treatments of a number of important contemporary philosophers, a series titled "The Library of Living Philosophers," a volume dedicated to Buber was completed in 1963. It included essays by recognized scholars as well as providing the opportunity for Buber's response. The section "Replies to My Critics" (1967c, 689–744) includes a few pages where Buber refers to his *Eclipse of God*. Once again, the Holocaust is not mentioned, but the issue of God's silence is paramount. He begins by reiterating the thesis of that book, quoting lines about how the "I-It relation, gigantically swollen ... steps in between and shuts off from us the light of heaven" (715–716). Buber adds that the Bible knows of the other side of this eclipse, "the divine side," which it metaphorically calls "the hiding of God, the veiling of the divine countenance." He continues,

> These last years in a great searching and questioning, seized ever anew by the shudder of the now, I have arrived no further than that I now distinguish a revelation through the hiding of the face, a speaking through the silence. The eclipse of God can be seen with one's eyes, it will be seen.
>
> (716)

Some issues raised in the secondary literature

There is an extensive literature on the philosophical investigations of the Holocaust by Heschel and Buber.[8] However, the body of commentary is bereft of discussions of the two philosophers together, which is surprising in light of some deep similarities in their life-experiences and fundamental religious views.[9] Three overlapping issues from the individual treatments will be pursued: the claim that each philosopher basically ignored the challenges posed by the Holocaust; the question whether there was any development in their thinking; the criticism that their examinations were not consistent and systematic.

Until recently, both Heschel and Buber were criticized for not seriously addressing the philosophical issues raised by the Holocaust. Thus, a significant twentieth-century Jewish philosopher, Emil Fackenheim, wrote, "Jewish thinkers of unquestionable Jewish authenticity such as Martin Buber and Abraham J. Heschel said little about the Holocaust—and that little with great reticence" (1982, 194). In harmony with this view is Morris Faierstein's statement, "The impression that one might gain from recent studies of the late Professor Abraham Joshua Heschel and his writings is that the Holocaust was not central to his theological thought" (1999, 255),[10] and also David Glantz's view that "it is surprising to realize how disrespectful is Buber of this subject [the Holocaust]" (quoted in Forman-Barzilai 2003, 175).

However, in light of the extensive periods and intensive intellectual probing covered by the preceding brief review of selected responses by Heschel and Buber, it is difficult to agree with this criticism of their lack of attention to the Holocaust. Both figures have forcefully spoken of being obsessed with the horrifying events. In an interview, Heschel confided, "Auschwitz and Hiroshima never leave my mind. Nothing can be the same after that" (quoted in Kaplan 1996, 117). Buber once disclosed to his life-long friend and biographer, Maurice Friedman, that beginning in 1945 and 1946, when he became aware of the full extent of the atrocity, and continuing "[f]or the rest of his life ... not an hour passed in which he did not think of the Holocaust" (Friedman 1988, 306).

More recently, a number of fine essays and larger works have documented each thinker's confrontation with the Holocaust. Critics such as Morris Faierstein, Edward Kaplan, and Robert Eisen have pointed to Heschel's often overlooked Yiddish works as additional evidence of his continual wrestling with that horror. Jerry Lawritson and David Forman-Barzilai have chronicled the different positions that Buber assumed in the struggle to salvage his notion of dialogue given his awareness of God's silence. Lawritson concluded, "The conception of the eclipse of God ... occupied Buber from 1939 until his death in 1965" (1996, 301).

A second issue arising from the critical literature concerns the question whether there was any clear development in their responses to the Holocaust. Steven Katz, in his "Abraham Joshua Heschel and Hasidism" (1980), definitely finds that *A Passion for Truth* constitutes a dramatic departure for Heschel. He writes,

> Heschel, to whose earlier works one could rightly apply the description of an earlier Jewish sage [Spinoza]—"the God-intoxicated philosopher"—now seems aware of quite another, altogether more absurd, dimension of human existence. ... This latter reflection ["that ultimately God Himself was responsible for the inherent falsehood of

human existence"] would be daring for any Jewish thinker, for Heschel it is revolutionary.

(97)

Katz's view of the revolutionary nature of Heschel's last book is, to me, unassailable. While Heschel had offered a number of different answers to the questions posed by the Holocaust—the responsibility of humans, the power still to accomplish good in the world, that there was "meaning beyond absurdity," that God shares in human suffering—there was no noticeable progression. With *A Passion for Truth*, even though all of these answers appear once again, they are not forwarded with the usual assuredness. Heschel for the last time weighed the challenges, and while he still saw faith as overcoming if not conquering these, his voice certainly wavered.

With Buber, the secondary literature is not able to clearly identify either progression or a final turning point in his reflections on the Holocaust. At times, the critics seem to hint at some development, but this may just be the outcome of an attempt to summarize Buber's positions. For example, Jerry Lawritson's "Martin Buber and the Shoah" (1996) suggests that there are three aspects in Buber's treatment of the "eclipse of God." There is first the "ontological" dimension, which includes both the apotheosis of the human subject and God's hiding His face. God's silence, including some possible speaking through the silence, is regarded by the author as a second aspect. The third is identified as "staying with God" (305). Forman-Barzilai summarizes Buber's efforts to understand the Holocaust in terms of the eclipse of God, God's hidden face, and the notion of speaking through the silence. He does hint at some development when he writes that "we observe signs that Buber abandoned the bold and secure foundational statements about God that had previously dwelled at the core of his philosophical system" (2003, 172).

I agree with the comments of the two critics, and others, that there is no clear progression in Buber's treatment of the Holocaust. The "Dialogue between Heaven and Earth" (1967b), originally delivered in 1950, already includes most of the major elements in Buber's repertoire: history appearing empty of God; God hiding Himself; humans being left with contending with God and waiting for a future manifestation of "our cruel and merciful Lord" (225). Buber's feature of God's "eclipse" is added soon after. His "Replies" (1967c) does introduce the note of "a revelation through the hiding of the face" (716), but what that means is left completely open.

Lastly, in the literature on Heschel and Buber comments are often made about the lack of consistent, systematic, and convincing answers in their treatments of the Holocaust. This is the case even with very sympathetic critics. In terms of Heschel, for example, in the course of his article, Katz questions the "philosophical coerciveness" and "logic" of some of his arguments and assertions, and hints at the need for more critical, detailed scrutiny overall (1980, 100, 102, 104). In reviewing Buber's "Dialogue between Heaven and Earth," Fackenheim writes that "this answer [that we contend with God and await His voice], arresting and thought-provoking in many ways, is, in one sense, no answer at all" (1982, 197). Forman-Barzilai is at one point more severe with Buber, stating that in "the philosophical and theoretical realm … Buber seems to move uneasily from one idea to another and his message seems hesitant, inconsistent, and often self-contradictory" (2003, 158).

Yet the same critics, and others, recognize that the Holocaust elicits no simple answer and that the struggles of these two philosophers evidence sincere religious responses. Katz follows his philosophical suspicion of one of Heschel's statements with the comment that it needs to be taken as a "confession of faith," and that "what is particularly impressive about it … is its total commitment. It is a religious position unalloyed by compromise" (1980, 100). Edward Kaplan continues in this appreciative vein,

> Heschel refuses to systematize the unspeakable—whether it be the divine Presence, God's silence at our agony or massive evil. As is faith itself, trust in God is not static, like a formulated creed, but an unending challenge, a way of thinking about nothing less than redemption.
>
> (1996, 130)

While Fackenheim found great lapses in Buber's answers to the Holocaust, he saw that it was not because Buber ignored its tests, writing, "Buber's thought was, despite all, shaken by the Holocaust, and this not at its political periphery but rather at what may be called its religious center" (1982, 196). Forman-Barzilai coins the term "agonism," as in "agonism *in* faith … means that the very notion of faith *itself* is being lived in agony over the very *visible* and undoubtedly perplexing ways of God" (2003, 171). He appreciated Buber's efforts in refusing "to give up his faith or admit defeat, to admit that whatever he lived and believed, wrote and fought for, was proven wrong by Hitler's satanic deeds" (172).

How does one reconcile this mixture of critical and laudatory statements in the secondary literature? The critics, as their philosophical subjects themselves, are mired in that situation of tension between an expectation or at least desire for an answer, for at least rational consistency, and the acknowledgement that reason and logic are overwhelmed by the extent and horror of this event. Kaplan clearly agrees with Heschel when writing, as we just saw, "Heschel refuses to systematize the unspeakable" (1996, 130), and later adds, "Even faith cannot untie the Gordian knot" (131). For Forman-Barzilai the notion of "agonism *in* faith" precisely characterizes not only Buber's response to the Holocaust, but "a new stage in human religiosity … in the face of God's mysterious (read: unknown) ways" (2003, 171).

Heschel and Buber are adamant that there is neither answer to nor comfort for the suffering in the Holocaust. Even in the wake of celebrating the reuniting of the city of Jerusalem in 1967, Heschel exclaimed, "And yet, there is no answer to Auschwitz" even if "Israel enables us to bear the agony of Auschwitz without radical despair" (1969, 115). Buber also does not see an answer forthcoming, neither from humans nor from God. He turns to Job's story, with the counsel not to expect "God to make a confession" or "explain his secrets" (2003a, 173).

Finally, what is absent from the secondary literature is the recognition that many of the philosophical characteristics and problems that are identified in the writings of Heschel and Buber can be correlated with classic signs of emotional trauma, as described in Chapter 2. This would include: obsession with the horror ("never a day went by without thinking of it"), lack of consistency or development in approach, along with lack of any resolution ("there is no answer to Auschwitz"), the undermining of fundamental trust ("God himself might be to blame"), and struggling with the missing justice and meaning ("the cruel and merciful Lord"). In this case the two individuals escaped, but they lost family, friends, and homeland. The "trauma of Auschwitz" is expressed through a philosophical medium, rather than conveyed bodily, through physical and psychological symptoms.

Comparing their responses

So, then, what distance actually separates the positions of Heschel and Buber? The perusal of the secondary literature has already noted one significant feature they had in common—that there was no closure to their wrestling with the Holocaust. There are other, more specific, overlaps discernable. One was the necessity for political action in the support of human rights and dignity. Their common theoretical considerations included: the ultimate responsibility for the Holocaust rests with humans; ours is a time of God's withdrawal or hiding His face; God and ultimate meaning are correlates for faith; speaking of God as a person has metaphoric value; faith requires a trust that does not limit God to human desires or measures of justice; the event of the Holocaust deeply impacts all reflections on theodicy. Of course, the comparison of any two thinkers' similarities will always show differences within them, but it is the shared that is the focus at this point.

Both Heschel and Buber were well known for social activism, which was an extension of their overall philosophies as well as part of their responses to the Holocaust. Heschel was a strident advocate concerning the civil rights of African-Americans, with the protest movement against the Vietnam War, and for the emigration of Jews persecuted in the Soviet Union. He regarded this work as authentically Jewish, in support of the dignity of life and against its satanic denial, exemplified by the Holocaust. Heschel considered prejudice, whether racial or religious, as being of one cloth, writing, "*Racial or religious bigotry* must be recognized for what it is: *satanism, blasphemy*" (1972, 86).

For Buber, the cause of reconciliation between Arabs and Jews in Palestine, and later in the State of Israel, was his most vital specifically political concern. He was instrumental in the formation of two organizations to bring understanding between Jews and Arabs and to advance his position of binationalism, *Brit Shalom* (the covenant of peace) in 1925 and *Ihud* or unity in 1942. Although his attention to this issue—"the Arab Question"—antedates the Holocaust, Buber recognized the influence of Nazism in that chauvinism of the quest for power for its own sake that he saw being advocated by some radical supporters of a Jewish national homeland (Mendes-Flohr 1983, 291–292).[11] In another essay the link was put more starkly, that such limitless national egoism leads to acting in "the land of Israel like Hitler" (quoted in Forman-Barzilai 2003, 159).

Heschel and Buber shared the view that the Holocaust was first and foremost a question of human responsibility. In *Man Is not Alone* (1951), Heschel insists that it is folly to shift "the responsibility for man's plight from man to God, in accusing the Invisible though the iniquity is ours" (151). Humans have defied and betrayed God, which has led to his departure, or as Heschel expresses it, "He was expelled. *God is in exile*" (153). This theme is not lost in Heschel's later works, so that even in the anguishing *A Passion for Truth* (1974), the main message is about recognizing and combating *human* falsehood and self-deception. In this connection Heschel says that the Holocaust "had its origin in a lie. ... Decimate the Jews and all problems would be solved" (321).

Buber expressed a similar accusation about human responsibility in the language of "the mastery and the rule" of the "I-It relation, gigantically swollen" (1952, 129). Here human self-interest and aggrandizement has obscured the ever-continuing voice of God. This notion of "the eclipse of God," fully detailed in the book of that name in 1952, is reiterated over a decade later, as we have seen, in Buber's "Replies to My Critics" (1967c, 715). The essay "Genuine Dialogue and the Possibilities of Peace" (1999, 195–202), shows another dimension of Buber's understanding of the human guilt for the Holocaust. In it he speaks of a coming "final battle of *homo humanus* against *homo contrahumanus*" (196). *Homo humanus* stands for those who believe in the possibilities of genuine dialogue, and speak directly with the intention of affirming and confirming the other. Opposed to them are those in league with the antihuman, who seek to exacerbate and profit from human divisions. Buber held that some persons in the camp of *homo contrahumanus*, who "have so radically removed themselves from the human sphere, so transposed themselves into the sphere of monstrous inhumanity" (195), were precisely the leaders and perpetrators of the Holocaust.

Following the common indictment of human responsibility, Heschel and Buber do speak of God's absence during that time and afterward. One way of portraying this absence is through the metaphor of God hiding. They share more than just this metaphor, including the idea that God's hiding is at least partially a reaction to humans turning from God. The most relevant piece in Heschel's work is, obviously, his chapter "The Hiding God" (1951, 151–157). It is here that he begins by criticizing those who see the Holocaust as a fundamentally theological problem, yet he does examine the splintered relationship to God. Taking his lead from a number of sources in the biblical text, Heschel contends that God was forced into exile because of human wickedness, malice, and cruelty. He argues that God is not by nature hidden, but He has been forced into exile by human actions. Referring to the prophet Isaiah, he writes,

> It is not God who is obscure. It is man who conceals Him. His hiding from us is not in His essence: "Verily Thou are a God that hidest Thyself, O God of Israel, the Savior!" (*Isaiah* 45:15). A hiding God, not a hidden God. He is waiting to be disclosed, to be admitted into our lives.
>
> (153–154)

We have already noted Buber's discussion of God hiding in "The Dialogue between Heaven and Earth" (1967b, 214–225). He writes of times when this dialogue is interrupted, referring to *Isaiah* 8:17, which describes a situation where God "hideth His face from the house of Jacob" (222), and seems totally absent from human affairs. At least in this context, Buber does not speak of human evil as the cause of hiding, referring for example to the slavery in Egypt, and to a story from *Psalm 82* about a time when God's angels misruled the earth (223). The letter to Ernsz Szilagyi adds to this that "He will not stop being the hidden God [the last words in Hebrew], when He reveals Himself anew" (2003a, 173), in the sense that God will not apologize or provide answers for his inaction. Finally, there is also Buber's reference to "a revelation through the hiding of the face, speaking through the silence" (1967c, 716).

One of the types of inconsistencies noted in the critical literature arises in the course of Buber's reflections on the hiding God. In "Dialogue between Heaven and Earth" (1967b), Buber distinguishes God's continual revelation in nature from that plane of history where "revelation is essentially not a continuous process, but breaks in again and again upon the course of events" (221–222). Yet, in "Replies" (1967c) he affirms, "I cannot conceive of any interruption of the divine revelation," and he does not seem to refer to the dimension of nature for he adds that still there is "a condition that works on us as a silence of God" (716). I cannot find a way to reconcile the two statements concerning whether revelation is continuous or discontinuous in history, and both are actually in harmony with other views he espoused.

In response to God's hiding or silence, both philosophers speak of a faith or trust in God that may have to transcend our reason or understanding. In *Heavenly Torah* (2007), Heschel uses the example of Rabbi Akiva to argue that where human suffering is clearly not the result of sin, God's justice can still be upheld, because it may serve the cause of purging the righteous person of some minor imperfection, or bring about a deeper intimacy with God. Heschel's *A Passion for Truth* (1974) echoes with a particular definition of faith: "Faith comes about in a collision of an unending passion for Truth and the failure to attain it by one's own means" (302).[12] The title of one section, "Meaning beyond Absurdity," underscores his belief that "the ultimate meaning of God's ways is not invalidated because of man's incapacity to comprehend it" (293).

Buber speaks of a waiting for God's reappearance based upon the faith in God's justice, even though this may exceed human understanding or desire. In very personal terms he writes, "My faith in you is not dependent on your doing what I see as just but in the fact that all your deeds are the just, more so, the absolute justice" (2003a, 172–173). This is true even when God's creation appears "frightening" and his acts "barbarous." Limiting faith to one's own image of the divine is for Buber nothing less than idolatry: "If someone accepts him otherwise [than as He is], he accepts a statue, an idol crafted by his own hand, a 'good' one that is easy to love" (173).

A few further common features will conclude this examination of similarities in the responses of Heschel and Buber to the Holocaust. The first is that the metaphor of God as person stands at the foundation of their various considerations. For Heschel, beyond the pronouns—exclusively male in both his and Buber's writing—God seeks human partners, commands and addresses them, is sometimes silent, shares human suffering, and even needs human comfort. The last is poignantly expressed, "When man is in distress, there is a cry of anguish in Heaven. God needs not only sympathy and comfort but partners, silent warriors" (1974, 300).

Buber's notion of God as a person resonates throughout his *I and Thou* (1970), as well as his deliberations on the Holocaust. In the former, he speaks of God "as the absolute person," who "enters into a direct relationship to us human beings through creative, revelatory, and redemptive acts, and thus makes it possible for us to enter into a direct relationship to him" (181). In relation to the Holocaust, this direct relationship to "Him" opens the way for Buber's discussion of trust, of waiting for an appearance, and especially, of His silence: "The other, the divine side, is called in the holy books of Israel the hiding of God, the veiling of the divine countenance. Nothing more than such an anthropomorphic image seems to be granted us" (1967c, 716). For both philosophers, drawing upon human relations to address the challenges of the Holocaust enables their responses to have the range, vitality, depth, and tone of sincerity that they have.

Additionally, Heschel and Buber argue that our very existence as humans requires a clinging to God, even following the Holocaust, because without God there is no authentic human existence. Heschel expresses this insight succinctly, in terms of meaning: "Expectation of meaning is an *a priori* condition of our existence;" and follows this with the postulate or "premise" that "God and meaning, as we understand them, are one" (1974, 290). Buber provides a more extended discussion, in a similar but different key, focusing on trust rather than meaning. This is presented in two of his essays in *A Believing Humanism* (1999). He holds that only through true speech between persons can *homo humanus*, humans in their fullest sense, come into existence. What true speech requires is trust in the other; even the stranger or enemy can be trusted when one addresses them with sincerity and respect. However, trust in the other is itself ultimately grounded in faith or trust in life, or Being, or, as Buber prefers, God. He writes,

> Here humanity and faith ... they penetrate each other, they work together, indeed, they are so centrally related to each other that we may say our faith has our humanity as its foundation and our humanity has our faith as its foundation.
>
> (117)

> It is simply trust that is increasingly lost to men in our time. And the crisis of speech is bound up with the loss of trust in the closest possible fashion, for I can only speak to someone in the true sense of the term if I expect him to accept my word as genuine. ... This lack of trust in Being [or God], this incapacity for unreserved intercourse with the other, points to an innermost sickness of the sense of existence.
>
> (201)

Finally, at least implicit in the discussions of Heschel and Buber is the dawning awareness that the Holocaust must have a central place in all Jewish reflections on human evil and God's justice, on the sufferings of the righteous and the innocent in history. As the first prominent Jewish philosophers to wrestle with the implications of this terror, they laid the groundwork for the role that the Holocaust would come to hold not only in relation to the issue of theodicy, but also for modern Jewish philosophical understandings of Jewish identity, the covenant with God, and the significance of the state of Israel. As demonstrated in their readings of Isaiah and Job, and in Heschel's examinations of rabbis Ishmael and Akiva, the Besht, and the Kotzker, the Holocaust's impact often extends even to contemporary reception of Judaism's classic sources.

Obviously, there are also important *differences* between the positions of Heschel and Buber, elements that are distinctive to each philosopher. With Heschel, this includes his discussions of divine pathos, that the major task remains to obey, and the promise of a messianic redemption. The first two of these features in Heschel's response to the Holocaust are already adumbrated in the prior exchange with Buber in the third decade of the twentieth century. As indicated earlier, Heschel's portrait of the biblical Prophets highlighted their access to God's inner life, which reveals God's passionate concern for and sharing of human emotions from love to anguish.[13] Heschel has written that "He is *both* transcendent beyond human understanding, *and* full of love, compassion, grief or anger" (quoted in Chester 2005, 143). Among numerous examples of what the notion of divine pathos provides is the story that Heschel tells at the end of that crucial section, "The Kotzker and Job" (1974, 263–303), of his final book. In a meeting between two Jews in a train, one person justified his action of saying his morning prayers, despite the Holocaust, with the line, "It suddenly dawned upon me to think how lonely God must be; look with whom He is left. I felt sorry for Him" (303). Here God is affected by human actions, in that He feels lonely, and humans can share and even comfort God through their prayers. These elements of intense intimacy between the divine and human partners—often classically portrayed in terms of a bridegroom and bride—not surprisingly resound with Heschel's background and participation in Hasidism. Buber's distance from this portrayal by Heschel of the accessibility to God's inner life can be gauged from some lines in "Dialogue between Heaven and Earth" (1967b). In what can be used as a direct rejoinder by Buber, he writes, "It [the Bible] does not deal with the essence of God but with His manifestation to mankind. The reality of which it treats is that of the human world" (220).

A Passion for Truth (Heschel 1974) also provides fine examples for other distinctive features. The story of "Barrels Full of Holes" (285–289) reiterates the refrain that one has a duty to obey the king, that is, to follow God's commands. Heschel writes, "The supreme category accessible to man, then, is that of command. And the supreme response of which man is capable is obedience" (289). This is an allusion to the continuing significance of Jewish law, which is a perennial theme in Heschel's treatment of Judaism. On the other hand, Buber, who was not a practicing Jew, never saw Jewish law as a vital dimension of modern Jewish life. It was for him a human-made and even fossilized feature of traditional Judaism that was no longer viable as a bridge to God. For example, *Halakhah* was a contentious issue that arose in a famous exchange between Buber and his friend Franz Rosenzweig. In a letter of 1924 to Rosenzweig, he writes, "I told you that for me, though man is a law-receiver, God is not a law-giver, and therefore the Law [*Halakhah*] has no universal validity for me" (Glatzer 1955, 115).

Heschel's references to God's heavenly reward and to messianic redemption in his repertoire of considerations concerning God, the Holocaust, and theodicy are also absent from Buber's work. In the story of the barrels, the wise laborer says, "Surely I am to be paid for every barrel!" (Heschel 1974, 286). This may allude to rewards in this life, to the doctrine of reward and punishment in the life to come, as well as to the final redemption in the messianic end of times. In terms of the latter, Heschel writes, "Our present order is but tentative; at the end of days, in the messianic era, there will be an end to mendacity and violence, as also to death" (299). Additionally, in *Heavenly Torah* (2007), through an analysis of the views of Rabbi Akiva, Heschel answers the question of why the just suffer. He holds that such "afflictions" deepen the contact with God, and that the suffering of innocents purges them of the little evil they have committed in order to hasten their entry into heaven (135). None of these ideas were serviceable to Buber, who was reticent to go beyond his statement that, whether in reference to the Bible, religion in general, or Judaism in particular, "the reality of which it treats is that of the human world" (1967b, 220).

Buber's distinctive response draws its resources from his dialogical philosophy. This philosophy, beginning with the poetic vision originally laid out in *I and Thou* (1970), almost sings of that encounter between humans and the "eternal Thou." Buber portrays a relationship of mutuality and reciprocity in which each participant stands in their fullness, and whose central element is language (57). This encounter is also the source of that cacophony of metaphors Buber uses to address the breakdown of the "dialogue between heaven and earth" (1967b, 214) at the time of and following the Holocaust: speech, eclipse, hiding, silence, waiting, and speaking through the silence.

In relation to Heschel's deliberations, three of these distinctive metaphors stand out. Buber's well-known terminology of the "eclipse of God" allows him to maintain his theme of God's eternal speech, and yet still note its frightening interruption, because human "selfhood that has become omnipotent ... steps in between and shuts off from us the light of heaven" (1952, 129). Humans are left, first of all, with a difficult if not terrible waiting, in response to which he laments, "The estrangement has become too cruel, the hiddenness too deep" (1967b, 224). It may be that the situation of Buber's waiting for a renewal of the dialogue with heaven is more extreme than we find in Heschel. This is because Buber does not have the comfort of sensing the divine presence through the practice of *Halakhah* or of the promises of heavenly reward and messianic redemption. As a consequence of the experience of God in these last years as "frightening" and his acts as "barbarous" (2003a, 173), the future is not unambiguous, even when the waiting is over. Buber leaves us with the haunting description, "Though His coming appearance resemble no earlier one, we shall recognize again *our cruel and merciful Lord*" (1967b, 225; my emphasis).

Still, Buber struggles to offer some hope even today, in his last lines, of "a revelation through the hiding of the face, a speaking through the silence" (1967c, 716). What type of gift is this? It is perhaps suggesting that if dialogue is a dance, then silence can be seen as one of its steps and not its end; or, following through with his metaphors, if in conversation speech at one point comes to a halt—silence breaks into the conversation—that silence itself can communicate, can have many meanings.

Finally, Buber's response to the Holocaust also differs from Heschel's in that he can describe the very specific ways that the breakdown in the divine–human dialogue affects interhuman relations, that is, what the impact of God's hiding and silence are for the "word" given and received between persons. The parallel between the divine–human and interhuman relationships is well expressed in Buber's "Afterword" (1970, 171–182) to *I and Thou*. He declares, "The central significance of the close association of the relation to God with the relation to one's fellow-men ... is my most essential concern" (171). In *A Believing Humanism* (1999), as we saw, Buber ties the lack of trust in God to the cessation of trust and genuine speech between persons: "This lack of trust in Being, this incapacity for unreserved intercourse with the other, points to an innermost sickness of the sense of existence" (201).

Not "Any Tom, Dick, and Harry"

We are now in the position to return to Heschel's statement about Buber's position and to offer an assessment. Heschel writes,

> Martin Buber's declaration "Nothing can make me believe in a God who punishes Saul because he did not murder his enemy" must be contrasted with the Kotzker's statement "A God whom any Tom, Dick and Harry could comprehend, I would not believe in."
>
> (1974, 292–293)

The meaning of the statement is clarified by its context. Directly antecedent we find: "It is a mistake to start with a human model and then seek to accommodate God to it" (292). Following it he writes that "the ultimate meaning of God's ways is not invalidated because of man's incapacity to comprehend it" (293), and soon quotes the famous lines from the prophet Isaiah (55:8f): "For My thoughts are not your thoughts, and your ways are not My ways. ... For as the Heavens are higher than earth, so are My ways higher than your ways, and My thoughts than your thoughts" (295).

Heschel's reference appears to be to one of Buber's reports, titled "Samuel and Agag," of a meeting in his "Autobiographical Fragments" (Buber 1967a, 31–33). Buber speaks of a discussion with an acquaintance on a train—repeating a setting Heschel also uses—that at one point turned to a biblical story in *I Samuel* 15. Here God has Samuel tell Israel's first king, Saul, that he will be stripped of the leadership position because he failed to obey the command of God and spared the life of the Amalekite commander, Agag. Buber tells his partner that "I have never been able to believe that this is a message of God. I do not believe it" (31), and later comments in the report that "nothing can make me believe in a God who punishes Saul because he has not murdered his enemy. And yet even today I still cannot read the passage that tells this otherwise than with fear and trembling" (33).

Heschel's criticism is that Buber is wrong to insist that God be limited to human judgments—in this case that of Buber—of what is desirable or what constitutes justice.[14] Doing this reduces the transcendent God to just an extension of the human.[15] Heschel's focus on Buber's reaction to this biblical episode is appropriate because it is both a good reflection of Buber's understanding of the divine–human relation, and it shows a revealing difference in their positions. Buber could not accept that God would command the death of a person and then punish Saul's noncompliance. It would undermine Buber's commitment to dialogue, to the centrality of the I–Thou relationship in the redemption of human and all of life.[16] This was a line he could not cross, even as he counseled an awaiting for the Presence of that "cruel and merciful Lord."

However, a final assessment of Heschel's critique must take more into account than this initial consideration. Is Buber guilty of reducing God to a human image? As we have seen, Buber argued directly against such a position, writing at times in the first person:

> "You [God] are the truth." ... I accepted you the way you are and you cannot make me doubt it. All I want is that you will be what you are and that you are what you are. My faith in you is not dependent on your doing what I see as just but in the fact that all your deeds are the just, more so, the absolute justice. ... If someone accepts him otherwise [than as He is], he accepts a statue, an idol crafted by his own hand, a "good" one that is easy to love.
>
> (2003a, 172–173)

This was also his lesson in reference to the book of *Job*, which ends not with some explanation of God's justice, but just with His appearance (1967b, 224).[17]

In turning back to Buber's report of the conversation with an acquaintance, it is interesting to see that the reference to Saul may not be the central lesson or the reason he included it in the "Autobiographical Fragments." He explains his rejection of the biblical story with the statement that "Samuel has misunderstood God" (1967a, 32). He also follows it with a reflection about translation. Buber writes, and the report itself ends with,

> And yet even today I still cannot read the passage that tells this otherwise than with fear and trembling. But not it alone. Always when I have to translate or to interpret a biblical text, I do so with fear and trembling, in an inescapable tension between the word of God and the words of man.
>
> (33)

Thus, Buber sees the Samuel–Saul episode as a lesson about a misunderstanding between God and Samuel, and about that difficulty in interpreting God's word that permeates the whole Bible itself. Buber comments further,

> What is involved is the fact that in the work of throats and pens out of which the text of the Old Testament has arisen, misunderstanding has again and again attached itself to understanding, the manufactured has been mixed with the received. We have no objective criterion for the distinction; we have only faith—when we have it.
>
> (32–33)

Buber wrote many times that while humans are addressed by God, it is up to them to interpret or understand what it means (1952, 98–99). God does not give direct commands. In this regard it is important to note that Heschel was himself no biblical literalist, writing in his major work, *God in Search of Man* (1955), that "as a report about revelation the bible itself is *a midrash*" (185), that is, an interpretation.[18]

Yet, the main message of Buber's story seems to be something different than the statement about not believing God would punish Saul, or even his comments on interpreting the word of God and biblical translation. The story is about this meeting with his acquaintance, who is, significantly, "an observant Jew" (1967a, 32). When Buber expressed his judgment about the Samuel story, the dialogue partner originally seemed angry and almost threatening in his reply: "You do not believe it?" However, later, after pondering further, his face was "transformed" and Buber writes, "It [his countenance] lightened, cleared, was now turned toward me bright and clear. 'Well,' said the man with a positively gentle tender clarity, 'I think so too.'" Buber adds, and I believe these are the main points of the story,

> There is in the end nothing astonishing in the fact that an observant Jew of this nature, when he has to choose between God and the Bible, chooses God: the God in whom he believes; Him in whom he can believe. And yet, it seemed to me at that time significant and still seems so to me today.
>
> (32)

Buber includes this report of a meeting in his "Autobiographical Fragments"[19] because it provides two lessons that are especially important to him. The first is about the transformative possibilities of true speech, even in the original context of a rather heated disagreement. The second is that Buber always sees a tension between institutional religion with its static texts and doctrines, and living faith. As Buber understands it, his partner, when directly faced with this choice, made a decision based on his own experience, his own faith. From all we have seen in Heschel, although he might not frame the conflict in the same way, he would certainly take the side of living experience and faith.[20]

Thus, Heschel's critique of Buber is both correct and incorrect, revealing some important differences in their positions, as well as obscuring even more fundamental similarities. In the final analysis, Buber's subtle but intense struggle with the Holocaust does not reflect the deliberations of the proverbial "Tom, Dick, and Harry," but of a living person of faith. Buber's position, as is that of Heschel, is of a sincere person who recognizes that in the face of a generation's and a people's deepest challenge, faith is a gift that does not ease but intensifies one's anguishing battle for meaning. As a true challenge, the confrontation with the philosophic implications of the Holocaust was transformative. It brought both philosophers to positions that conflicted with their deeply held philosophies of "God in search of

man," and of "the dialogue between heaven and earth." In this vein, their
responses are reminiscent of Emmanuel Levinas' portrayal of the post-
Holocaust situation of both the protest against and intimacy with God,
beneath this, our often "empty sky" (1990, 143).[21] Their costly won insights
point to the true purpose and test of the best in modern Jewish philosophy,
which Hilary Putnam expresses through the title of his book *Jewish
Philosophy as a Guide to Life* (2008).

Notes

1 Briefly, there is no consensus in the use of or distinction between the terms
   "Jewish philosophy" and "Jewish theology" in either the primary or secondary
   literature of modern Jewish thought. The phrase "depth theology" plays an
   important part in Heschel's work, although his major work, *God in Search of
   Man*, carries the subtitle "A Philosophy of Judaism." Buber, however, offered
   both his original thinking and his many examinations of modern Western
   thought under the rubric of philosophy.
2 This article thus makes the claim that some familiarity with the life-histories
   of Heschel and Buber is necessary in arriving at a credible assessment of their
   responses to the Holocaust. I believe that while judgments about the philosophical coherence of their reflections should be made independently of such considerations, a fuller understanding of their positions requires an awareness of these
   biographical matters. In his *The Varieties of Religious Experience*, the philosopher and psychologist William James offers a similar approach (2004, 14–15).
3 The term "tremendum" is taken from Arthur Cohen's work *The Tremendum*
   (1981).
4 Buber's commitment to dialogue was more than a theoretical concern. For
   example, in his recent biography of Buber, Paul Mendes-Flohr illustrates the
   pivotal place of conversations with the social theorist Gustav Landauer in the
   development of Buber's thought. He writes,

   > Whatever transpired [in meetings over several days in 1916], it is evident
   > that their time together occasioned a radical transformation in Buber's
   > thinking. ... This transformation paved the way for his philosophy of dia-
   > logue, which would be formally inaugurated by the publication of *I and
   > Thou* in 1923.
   >
   > (2019, 108)

5 Robert Eisen presents a fine, extensive discussion of this work in his essay "A.
   J. Heschel's Rabbinic Theology as a Response to the Holocaust" (2003).
6 This is the position that Eisen offers (2003, 215–220).
7 Heschel's use of the Kotzker to examine the topic of God's responsibility for
   human evil is a major theme in Steven Katz's article "Abraham Joshua Heschel
   and Hasidism" (1980).
8 Of course, the secondary literature on the wider religious and philosophical
   responses to the Holocaust is extensive. Many thinkers have come to agree with
   Richard Rubenstein's early declaration,

   > I am convinced that the problem of God and the death camps is the central
   > problem for Jewish theology in the twentieth century. The one pre-emi-
   > nent measure of the adequacy of all contemporary Jewish theologies is

the seriousness with which they deal with this supreme problem of Jewish history.

(1966, 223)

A small representative selection of responses might include two edited selections, Michael Morgan's *The Holocaust Reader*, and John Roth and Michael Berenbaum's *Holocaust: Religious and Philosophical Implications*, as well as Steven Katz's *Post-Holocaust Dialogues*. Also see the discussion of Jewish responses in Chapter 4.

9 Even the book *Between Heschel and Buber* (Even-Chen and Meir 2012) does not compare their views about the Holocaust in detail.

10 Eisen writes, "Until recently, scholars have assumed that Abraham Joshua Heschel did not grapple seriously with the Holocaust" (2003, 211).

11 See many of Buber's writings on the Arab Question from 1918 to 1965 in *A Land of Two Peoples* (Mendes-Flohr 1983).

12 In typical Heschel fashion, this sentence, which comes in the last pages of the book, is itself a paragraph.

13 Eisen finds that the notion of divine pathos includes the idea that suffering affects God's very essence (2003, 216).

14 Emmanuel Levinas appears to support Heschel's position that Buber is wrong to reject the biblical story of Saul and Agag out of conscience. Levinas speaks of his "indignation ... that Buber thinks that his conscience knows more" about such matters than the Bible does (2001, 78; see also 73).

15 This interpretation of the meaning of Heschel's comment is in harmony with Katz's position (1980, 100–101). His article includes the most direct discussion of Heschel's criticism of Buber, although only one paragraph long, that I have found in the secondary literature.

16 There is also Fackenheim's serious claim that Buber had great difficulty in facing radical evil, evil for its own sake (1982, 195). In light of the material in the present article, Fackenheim's position is open to dispute.

17 Thus, even though the long quote above is from a private letter, it is in harmony with what Buber has offered in print.

18 Heschel also states just before that "the nature of revelation, being an event in the realm of the ineffable, is something which words cannot spell, which human language will never be able to portray" (1955, 184–185).

19 It is significant that Buber's "Autobiographical Fragments" were later published as a book, *Meetings: Martin Buber* (Friedman 1973).

20 Heschel frequently critiques official religious institutions, creeds, and dogmas. The last section, "The Kotzker Today," in A *Passion for Truth* uses the Rebbe to criticize many facets of contemporary Jewish life (1974, 307–323).

21 See also the author's chapter "Rosenzweig and Levinas: On Anthropomorphism, the Holocaust, and God's Presence" (Oppenheim 1997, 28–52).

4   Jewish philosophical perspectives on trust and trauma

The dialectic of trust in God and the trauma of the Holocaust pulses through the writings of many significant modern Jewish philosophers. The Hebrew word *emunah* can be translated as both faith and trust; the Jewish philosophers emphasize the connection with the latter. This is a major refrain in Martin Buber's book *Two Types of Faith*, where he portrays *emunah* as an "effective ... actual trust in God," stating, "By its very nature trust is substantiation of trust in the fullness of life in spite of the course of the world which is experienced" (2003b, 40).

However, this understanding of the nature of trust in God is not exclusive to Buber or to the other Jewish philosophers under review. The singular importance for both the individual and the community of trust in the Lord, *Adonai*, is the pervasive message of the Hebrew Bible itself. It appears repeatedly in the call and promise to Abraham, the covenant between the Jewish people and the Lord at Mt. Sinai, the history of the relationship between the people and God from the period of the Tribal Confederacy through the Monarchy (Deuteronomic history), the message of the Prophets, and most powerfully in the great *Psalm 23*: "Though I walk through the valley of the shadow of death, I will fear no evil for Thou art with me" (23:4). What scholars identify as one of the earliest written pieces in the biblical text, the covenant at Shechem in *Joshua* 24, is a template for this trust. Joshua begins the covenant ceremony by recalling the early encounters between the Jewish people and the Lord, including Abraham's call, Exodus, and the taking of the Land of Israel. This is the necessary precursor for the covenant. Two parties can only enter into an agreement if there is trust, and this trust grows out of the people's prior experience of God's guiding and saving presence.

Trust in the Jewish philosophers

The whole of Franz Rosenzweig's *The Star of Redemption* can be seen as an extensive exegesis on trust. The *Star* begins with the individual's paralyzing fear of death—"all that is mortal lives in this fear of death" (2005, 9)—and ends with a trust in life, because "Revelation teaches us to trust in the Creator, to await the Redeemer" (404). In the *Star*, God's transformational love, i.e., Revelation, refashions the isolated, fearful self into a trusting, confident soul open to the world. The core of that openness is the turning to others in love and responsibility, which is actualized in response to the divine commandment to love the neighbor. This is meta-phorically expressed in the *Star*: "Only the soul loved by God can receive the commandment of neighborly love so far as to fulfill it" (231). The trust that establishes a life of loving the neighbor and bringing together persons in community is reaffirmed in the concluding lines of the book:

> To walk humbly with your God—nothing more is asked for here than a wholly present trust. But trust is a great word. It is the seed from which faith, hope and love grow. ... To walk humbly with your God—the words are above the gate, the gate that leads ... into life.
>
> (447)

For Rosenzweig, human life requires a fundamental trust in order to flourish. This trust in life, in the meaningfulness of one's life and life overall, cannot be self-generated, or even emerge as the product of the purely interhuman. It has a divine origin. The categories of Creation, Revelation, and Redemption are signposts for a life guided by God's providence. Still, Redemption is actually a human project, for through fulfilling the commandment to love the neighbor moments of time ripen into instants of eternity (258–259). Thus, "Eternity is a future, which, without ceasing to be future, is nevertheless present" (241). This process of en-souling life gives both hope and meaning to what otherwise appears as the ceaseless and meaningless round of birth and death, of war and revolution.[1]

Two features of the transformed self are important in the present con-text: humility, as seen above, and language or speech. Rosenzweig writes of the former that humility is

> conscious of being what it is through the grace of a Higher Being. ... It knows that nothing can happen to it. And it also knows that no power can rob it of this consciousness. This consciousness carries humility wherever it might go.
>
> (2005, 181)

This sense of humility includes what is termed in the French language *amour propre*, or self-respect. Self-respect is not a type of egoism, rather it is a respect for oneself as a person, among other persons. For Rosenzweig, this virtue is not, once again, self-generated, but a hidden, uplifting gift from "a Higher Being."

Unlike many philosophers, Rosenzweig trusts language to express and communicate even the most sublime feelings and experiences. This trust relies on his view that language is both totally human and totally divine. *The Star of Redemption* poetically proclaims this in the context of God's creation. Language is described as "the wedding gift of the Creator to humanity," which is "the mutual possession of the children of men" (2005, 120). Being a gift implies that

> to trust it [language] is easy, for it is in us and around us, and when it comes to us from the "outside," nothing other than it echoes from our "inside" toward the "outside." The spoken word is the same, whether it is listened to or said. The ways of God and the ways of man are different, but the word of God and the word of man are the very same. What man feels in his heart as his own human language is the word that has come from the mouth of God.
>
> (163)

Rosenzweig's last written text, "A Note on [Biblical] Anthropomorphisms," augments the lessons given in the *Star*. Its main assertion is that the biblical text is as authentic and alive today as it was in the past, specifically that "we *are* entitled to a boundless trust in his [God's] unboundable powers" (1998, 140),

> that God is capable of what he wills (thus even of meeting the creature from time to time in fully bodily and spiritual reality) and that the creature is capable of what he should be (thus even of fully understanding and recognizing God's self-embodying or self-spiritualization from time to time turning toward him).
>
> (144)

Martin Buber's explanation of *emunah* cited earlier, "trust [in God] is substantiation of trust in the fullness of life" (2003b, 40), is fully consistent with Rosenzweig's presentation. In the pivotal section of *I and Thou*, Buber utilizes the concept of "meaning" to explain the main implication of this trust. Revelation, that is, the experience of and relation to the divine, furnishes

> the inexpressible confirmation of meaning. It is guaranteed. Nothing, nothing can henceforth be meaningless. The question about the meaning of life has vanished. ... The guarantee does not wish to remain shut up within me, it wants to be born into the world by me. ... The meaning we receive can be put to the proof in action only by each person in the uniqueness of his being and in the uniqueness of his life.
>
> (1970, 158–159)

Buber holds that the relationship to God provides a confirmation, guarantee, or trust in life, that is, in the meaningfulness of life. While the question about life's meaning is no longer present, it cannot be formulated into some specific piece of knowledge. This guarantee must be lived out by each person in her or his uniqueness. A later essay succinctly expresses these ideas: "He [God] addresses me about something that he has entrusted to me and that I am bound to take care of loyally" (1965, 45).

The interconnections between trust in God and both speech and relationships with others is explored in *A Believing Humanism*. Buber holds that only through true speech between persons can *homo humanus*, persons in their full dignity, flourish. What true speech requires is trust in the other, which is itself grounded in faith or trust in life (1999, 201). In all, a fundamental faith/trust in God, life, one's assigned place in the world, other persons, and speech are intrinsically interwoven:

> Here humanity and faith ... they penetrate each other, they work together, indeed, they are so centrally related to each other that we may say our faith has our humanity as its foundation and our humanity has our faith as its foundation.
>
> (117)

For Buber, as well as the other Jewish philosophers here, trust in God cannot evade the challenge posed by human mortality. Buber does not approach this topic utilizing traditional refrains about the immortality of the soul or the coming of the messiah. The very nature of trust in God is that it abides or even deepens despite the inability to utilize or even foresee an easy or established answer. The trust in the "absolute person" (1970, 181) who is God features the term "eternity":

> The genuine faith speaks: I know nothing of death, but I know that God is eternity, and I know this, too, that he is my God. Whether what we call time remains to us beyond our death becomes quite unimportant to us next to this knowing, that we are God's—who is not immortal, but eternal. Instead of imagining ourselves living instead of dead, we shall prepare ourselves for a real death which is perhaps the final limit of time but which, if that is the case, is surely the threshold of eternity.
>
> (1999, 231)

Mirroring Rosenzweig's discussion, a crucial feature of the trust in the divine is the notion that meaning abides or that nothing of real value is lost in eternity.

Abraham Joshua Heschel's writings over decades emphasize the closeness of God to humans and the human response of faith. While not often using the term trust, he explores the experience and implications of that trust in the divine. Heschel does write about faith, which for him concerns a living, fulfilling way of life. The correspondence between faith and trust comes across in a citation in one of his last works, *Heavenly Torah*. Describing the relationship to God, "the path of faith," he refers to the third century Talmudic scholar Rabbi Joshua ben Levi, who "expressed the view of many of his colleagues when he said, 'Whoever has faith in

God will merit becoming like Him, as it is written, "Blessed is the man who trusts in God and whose trust God is'" (Jeremiah 17:7)" (2007, 192).

One term that continually arises in Heschel's repertoire is "passion," vital to both the divine and human sides of their relationship. Particularly in his early book on the biblical prophets, he highlights the possibility of humans having some access to or experience of God's inner life: "He is *both* transcendent beyond human understanding, *and* full of love, compassion, grief or anger" (quoted in Chester 2005, 143). Passion was also the centerpiece of his well-known definition of faith, "Faith comes about in a collision of an unending passion for Truth and the failure to attain it by one's own means" (1974, 302). These statements underscore an understanding that he shared with Rosenzweig and Buber, that trust in God is not about attaining some deep knowledge or certainty, but refers to the full passionate life of a person.

Heschel also echoes the themes of hope and meaning. He sees the traditional hope for the final redemption in the messianic end of times as a vibrant part of the trust in God (1974, 299). He also understands that while the idea that there is meaning to human life is a core feature of the relationship to God, it is an expectation, that is, a fundamental way of looking at the world based on trust, and not some type of logical conclusion: "Expectation of meaning is an *a priori* condition of our existence"; and "God and meaning, as we understand them, are one" (290).

Trauma in the Jewish philosophers

There is a vast and ever expanding literature on what Arthur Cohen describes as that "ontological gathering of evil," that "abyss" or "caesura," which is the Holocaust (1981, 1).[2] This section will explore the philosophical challenges to retain some semblance of faith/trust in God in the face of what is often seen as the paradigmatic episode of collective trauma. Material from the earlier chapter on Abraham Heschel and Martin Buber will be reexamined in this effort, augmented by a few selected references to Emmanuel Levinas, Elie Wiesel, and Emil Fackenheim.[3] The lives of all of these thinkers were personally impacted by the Holocaust, in terms of being forced to flee the scourge, losing family and friends, and being incarcerated in a detention, prisoner of war, or concentration camp.

While the general problem of evil in a world created by God is an acute issue for both Heschel and Buber, they were obsessed with the horrifying events of the Holocaust. Heschel confides that "Auschwitz and Hiroshima never leave my mind. Nothing can be the same after that" (Kaplan 1996, 117), and it is said of Buber that "not an hour passed in which he did not think of the Holocaust" (Friedman 1988, 306). The impact of this event on Heschel and the other Jewish philosophers reviewed here is dramatically expressed in the lines: "Life in our time has been a nightmare for many of us, tranquility an interlude, happiness a fake. Who could breathe at a time when man was engaged in murdering the holy witness to God six million times?" (Heschel 1974, 300–301).

At times Heschel appears to despair of any rationalization or justification for this paramount evil. Still, he suggests that human suffering brings humans closer to God and even allows them to share in the divine pathos (2007, 135). Perhaps a note that ends with a deference to silence embodies Heschel's final struggles: "The shattering queries continue to come in such overwhelming cascade, the agonies pile up so dreadfully, that they rinse away the power to speak" (1974, 301).

While Buber's understanding of the traumatic consequences of the Holocaust does not reveal any progressive development, the severity of its challenge to the trust in God remains close to his heart. In this setting he laments, "The estrangement has become too cruel, the hiddenness too deep" (1967a, 224). Buber struggles with overlapping responses to this situation, each paradoxically acknowledging the damage to this trust and yet reaching out, hoping for some intangible relief. Utilizing the metaphorical richness of the notion of God as person, he probes, contests, prepares for, and reaffirms the relationship.

> [Probing:] These last years in a great searching and questioning, seized ever anew by the shudder of the now, I have arrived no further than that I now distinguish a revelation through the hiding of the face, a speaking through the silence. The eclipse of God can be seen with one's eyes, it will be seen.
>
> (1967b, 716)

> [Contesting:] No, rather even now we contend, we too, with God, even with Him, the Lord of Being, whom we once, we here, chose for our Lord. We do not put up with earthly being; we struggle for its redemption, and struggling we appeal to the help of our Lord, who is again and still a hiding one. In such a state we await His voice, whether it comes out of the storm or out of a stillness that follows it. Though His coming appearance resemble no earlier one, we shall recognize again our cruel and merciful Lord.
>
> (1967a, 225)

> [Preparing for:] How is a Jewish life after Auschwitz possible? Today I no longer know exactly what Jewish life is, and I am not sure it will be known to me in the future. But I know what it means to cling to Him. The ones who continue to cling to Him are pointing toward what could justly be called in the future Jewish life.
>
> (2003a, 173)

> [Reaffirming:] "You [God] are the truth." ... I accepted you the way you are and you cannot make me doubt it. All I want is that you will be what you are and that you are what you are. My faith in you is not dependent on your doing what I see as just but in the fact that all your deeds are the just, more so, the absolute justice. ... If someone accepts

> him otherwise [than as He is], he accepts a statue, an idol crafted by his own hand, a "good" one that is easy to love.
>
> (2003a, 172–173)

The preceding quotations vividly exhibit Buber's wrestling with the Holocaust. The notions of "revelation through the hiding" and "speaking through the silence" point to nothing concrete but to a naked hope for some divine presence. The characterization of God, "our cruel and merciful Lord," is frightening, exposing that Buber at least to some real extent attributes the absence to God. Is this at all mitigated by the possessive "our"? Among expressions contesting God's actions, Buber asserts that the Jewish people will remain steadfast, "cling." Finally, despite intensely conflicting feelings, Buber reaffirms God's justice as well his trust in the One with whom they have been betrothed through history.

A few brief references to other significant Jewish philosophic figures on the ramifications of the Holocaust reinforce and augment the central theme of salvaging some vestiges of trust following the trauma of the Holocaust. Emmanuel Levinas' extensive philosophical writings are a testament to those who died in the Holocaust as well as to all victims of racism (1981, v). He categorically rejects the notion that there is any meaning or purpose to the Holocaust, writing that the Holocaust is "the end of theodicy" (1998, 97). There is a human lesson in it, however: that the highest imperative is to listen for and respond to the voice of the stranger, poor, widow, and orphan, actually to the presence of every other person. The ethical demand from and inescapable responsibility for the other overrides every evasion and even self-concern.[4] While the suffering of the other can never be justified, i.e., it is without purpose or "useless," one's own suffering can have a meaning if it is taken as a call to attend to the other's plight. He writes,

> It is in the interhuman perspective of *my* responsibility for the other, without concern for reciprocity, in my call for his or her disinterested help, in the asymmetry of the relation of *one* to the *other*, that I have tried to analyze the phenomenon of useless suffering.
>
> (1998, 101)

Levinas still sees the relationship to God as both viable and relevant. The great range of Jewish experiences of God as a person opens the way for intense struggles with questions of trust, hope, and meaning. In the face of divine hiddenness and silence—what he designates as the present-day experience of an "empty sky" (1990, 143)—the human partner is entrusted to rebel against, demand an accounting from, as well as to love and find intimacy with the elusive divine spouse. Levinas embraces this paradox: "Loving the Torah [especially its message of love of the neighbor] even more than God means precisely having access to a personal God against Whom one may rebel—that is to say, for Whom one may die" (145).

Elie Wiesel was a famous survivor and literary chronicler of the Holocaust, fiction being his main *entrée* to that "madness on an absolute scale" (1979, 201). He insists that words are not capable of measuring or describing the horror of the event and that all the traditional paths to uphold God's justice in history are dead ends, concluding that "in truth, Auschwitz signifies ... the defeat of the intellect that wants to find a Meaning—with a capital *M*—in history" (2000, 71). Despite this, his novels and essays hint at what it means to stay with Him. In the brief reflection "God's Suffering: A Commentary," Wiesel portrays God as a father who "accompanies his children into exile" (1995, 103). The traumatic pain of the Holocaust can never be wiped away, but there is some relief in sharing it within a millennia-old companionship: "What happens to us touches God. What happens to Him concerns us. We share in the same adventure and participate in the same quest. We suffer for the same reasons and ascribe the same coefficient to our common hope" (103–104).

The philosopher Emil Fackenheim often mentions Wiesel in his deliberation on the Holocaust. He rejected the possibility of any conclusive meaning or answer to what he termed "the trauma of the Holocaust" (1978: 72). His response focuses on the notion of *midrash*, a term that means commentary and is customarily applied to Jewish philosophy as well as to interpretive stories. However, Fackenheim determines that even traditional *midrash* is not an adequate guide to the unique evil of the Holocaust. He writes of its evil on an absolute scale: "But the Holocaust calls into question not this or that way of being human, but *all* ways. It ruptures civilizations, cultures, religions, not within this or that social or historical context, but within *all possible* contexts" (1982, 262).

In the vein of "mad midrash," Fackenheim provides literary offerings and a commanding praxis (1978, 265–269). Since no single, coherent response is possible, two of his stories outline a halting effort. First, he writes of a "commanding Voice of Auschwitz" that could be heard following the event, and later that God's partial *Tikkun* or redemption was already evidenced in the heroic efforts of men and women at that time to resist the Nazis by affirming their own humanity (Morgan 1987, 168, 187–188). The Jewish praxis, which follows from the first story, is to reaffirm one's tie to Judaism and the Jewish people: "For a Jew after Auschwitz, only one thing is certain: he may not side with the murderers and do what they have left undone" (179). The second praxis, working to redeem the world, is incumbent on everyone. In Fackenheim's words, reaffirming the path taken by the heroic victims of the Holocaust noted above, "*A Tikkun, here and now, is mandatory for a Tikkun, then and there, was actual*" (1982, 254, italics in original).

Résumé, Jewish philosophers

In the treatment of trust and trauma in the work of these selected modern Jewish philosophers, a number of themes and issues can be highlighted.

There is a clear correlation between the main features or even powers of trust and the direct assault that the trauma of the Holocaust inflicted. Among the particular subjects that arise on both sides of this clash are: meaning, hope, narrative, language, God as person, and the underlying notion of intersubjectivity.

For many religious thinkers and practitioners in the three biblical traditions, the essence of the relationship to God is attributed to the term "faith." Faith in this context is often linked with "belief," as in the belief in some idea or doctrine. However, this association does not do justice to the full effects in a life, including the interpersonal, that the Jewish philosophers attribute to the existential impact of trust in God. This passionate "trust in," lived out in the everyday, extends to the self, other persons, the world, and God.

Rosenzweig uses the term "humility" to describe some dimensions of the trust in the self that arises out of the God relation and believes that this quality is the "seed from which faith, hope, and love grow" (2005, 447). Trust in other persons is addressed in a number of ways. Those whom one encounters in the midst of life are, without exception, included under the rubric of the "neighbor." The nature of that relationship is prescribed by the divine command to love the neighbor, which Levinas interprets in terms of an inescapable and inexhaustible responsibility for the other. For Buber, Rosenzweig, and Levinas the trust in the other as well as in language are adjuncts of the primary trust in God. Hence Rosenzweig's "What man feels in his heart as his own human language is the word that has come from the mouth of God" (163).

Trust in the world is directly addressed by Buber through his equation of "trust in God" with "trust in the fullness of life" (2003b, 40). The term "meaning" is also relevant here, what Buber sees as "the meaning of life" (1970, 159). While indefinable, this corollary of revelation "is more certain for you than the sensations of your senses" (159). Rosenzweig explains this association as a result of the recipient of revelation gaining a fundamental orientation to life, guided by the categories of Creation, Revelation, and Redemption. Heschel encapsulates this point: "God and meaning, as we understand them, are one" (1974, 290).

What of the dual questions of God's accessibility and the substance of the trust? Rosenzweig turns to the biblical anthropomorphisms to evidence that God is capable of "meeting the creature from time to time in fully bodily and spiritual reality" and humans have the ability of "fully understanding and recognizing God's … from time to time turning toward" them (1998, 144). The content of God's revelation is, as we have seen, inexpressible, and consequently "no prescription" leads from the encounter (Buber 1970, 159). There is hope and promise, even in the face of death. However, hope and promise are tied to trust and not to knowledge or some defined content. At times, the philosophers speak of the end of history or messianic end, but they still leave the details to God. The doctrine of immortality of the soul might be more specific, but this idea plays no vital role in the thought of these philosophers.

Trust in God does not eliminate periods of doubt, especially in terms of the problem of evil, that perennial clash between confidence in God's justice and the inescapable realization that the world is haunted by violence and injustice. The Holocaust, with its "suffering of innocents" (Levinas 1990, 143), turned what was at times a personal and at other times perhaps an abstract confrontation with evil into a face-to-face traumatic encounter. The "agonism *in* faith" attributed to Buber—"the very notion of faith *itself* is being lived in agony over the very *visible* and undoubtedly perplexing ways of God" (Forman-Barzilai 2003, 171)—is equally applicable in describing the shock of the Holocaust in the life and thought of many Jewish philosophers of our time. For Buber, the confrontation with the Holocaust severely tested the main message of the "dialogue between heaven and earth" (1967a, 214), and for Levinas the dedication,

> To the memory of those who were closest among the six million assassinated by the National Socialists, and of the millions on millions of all confessions and all nations, victims of the same hatred of the other man, the same anti-semitism.
>
> (Levinas 1981, v)

was definitive from very early on.

In the wake of the Holocaust, there is a rupture in the foundational trust in God as well as in associated themes including meaning, hope, and language. Humans are recognized as those ultimately responsible, but God's inaccessibility is expressed through the metaphors of silence, hiddenness, and the "empty sky" (Levinas 1990, 143). The possibility of finding some purpose or meaning in history is condemned: The Holocaust signifies both "the end of theodicy" (Levinas 1998, 97) and the "defeat of the intellect that wants to find a Meaning—with a capital *M*—in history" (Wiesel 2000, 71).

The corruption of thought and language extends to everyday speech between persons as well as literary approaches through *midrash*. The first is lamented by Buber: "This lack of trust in Being [or God], this incapacity for unreserved intercourse with the other, points to an innermost sickness of the sense of existence" (1999, 201). The traditional Jewish *entrée* to situations of religious and existential crisis, narrative or *midrash*, is also shattered. What Fackenheim designates as post-Holocaust "mad midrash" (1978, 265) references the short stories and novels of Elie Wiesel, in which the lens of madness provides the singular vantage point to glimpse the new reality.

Hope has not been completely overthrown, but its dimensions are skewed. Its substance is ephemeral and even the object of the underlying trust is described in an anguishing tone: "Though His coming appearance resemble no earlier one, we shall recognize again our cruel and merciful Lord" (Buber 1967a, 225). What is left to the individual and the people is a covenantal existence of contest and appeal, protest and expectation, emptiness and intimacy, but also taking action. Levinas' response to the crisis is to see in the face of the other the sovereign command "Thou shalt not kill!" (2001, 61), that is, one's ultimate responsibility for the other. For Fackenheim, a prelude to a partial redemption or *Tikkun* was visible in the defense of human dignity during the Holocaust, and therefore its affirmation in the present is obligatory (1982, 254).

On religious language

This approach to religious language has a number of corollaries. The discussion of religious trust in terms of God as person, intersubjectivity, and meetings focuses on how the divine is experienced. It is not the language of metaphysical or scientific claims concerning ultimate reality, the nature of God, or even God's existence; it is fundamentally phenomenological. Stated in a different manner, the experiences of trust and trauma, mutuality and alienation, hope and despair can be understood and expressed in a variety of ways, one of which is the language of religious faith.[5]

This perspective, with its powers and limits, is explicitly addressed by Rosenzweig, Buber, and Levinas. In portraying the biblical anthropomorphisms, Rosenzweig insists that they "are throughout assertions about meetings between God and man. God is never described" (1998, 138). In analyzing a few stanzas from a biblical poem depicting how such a meeting was experienced, he finds that "every single declaration is only the one end of a line at whose other end stands the one praying, calling full of fear for help and who sees how God draws near to him" (139). The power of the lines lies in their affirmation that God can be trusted to accompany the individual even in the most trying situations. For many who genuinely experience the world in this way, any metaphysical assertion about the divine, including about God's existence or non-existence, rings hollow, bordering on being impertinent.

While Buber acknowledges that to use the language of God as person is a "contradiction," its meaning is vibrant for him:

> God ... enters into direct relationship to us human beings through creative, revelatory, and redemptive acts, and thus makes it possible for us to enter into a direct relationship to him. This ground and meaning of our existence establishes each time a mutuality of the kind that can obtain only between persons.
>
> (1970, 181)

Buber's understanding is that for those who experience the relationship to the divine, in "creative, revelatory and redemptive acts," as the "ground and meaning" of their existence, the notion of "mutuality" is crucial, and this can only apply "between persons." Still, Buber does not see his view as making some type of metaphysical claim: "The concept of personhood is, of course, utterly incapable of describing the nature of God" (181).

As with Rosenzweig and Buber, Levinas presents a sensitive and consistent view about what divine transcendence and infinity entail. These are
not attributes but function as expressions about the limits of human knowledge and the depths of human longing and experience. Levinas writes,
"For my part, I think that the relation to the Infinite is not a knowledge
but a Desire" (1985, 92). He describes desire in terms of something that
"cannot be satisfied," which "nourishes itself on its own hungers and is
augmented by its satisfaction" (92). Levinas means by this that the relation
to God is an unquenchable passion, "non-thematizable in thought" (106).

The love of the neighbor, that is, the responsibility to the other, is for
Levinas, as it is for Rosenzweig and Buber, the essence of religious life. It
is only in the grasp of that responsibility and in the process of its fulfill-
ment that there is meaning to the idea of a relationship to God. Levinas
draws upon the biblical performance of that responsibility, conveyed by
the Hebrew term *hineni*, in writing, "I will say that the subject who says
'Here I am!' [*hineni*] *testifies* to the Infinite. It is through this testimony,
whose truth is not the truth of representation or perception, that the revelation of the Infinite occurs" (1985, 106).

This overall understanding of religious language and the religious
life by the Jewish philosophers clearly clashes with some popular views
of these matters, and particularly as detailed in Chapter 1 in terms of
Benjamin's approach. Despite the references in *Beyond Doer and Done To*
to "neo-Platonic mysticism" and Kierkegaard (2018, 21), she maintains a
very disparaging attitude toward religion or at least biblical religions. In
her reference to "the Cain and Abel myth," of "only one can live" (2018,
230), she identifies religion with the splitting between the dignified and the
discarded. Earlier works correlate religion with the illusionary promise of
redemption in exchange for the believer's complete submission to absolute
authority (1988, 5, 60). In all, there is an underlying portrait of religion as
innately absolutist and exclusivist.

However, as consistently addressed here, both Rosenzweig and Buber
see the commandment to love the neighbor as fundamental to their
understanding of the nature of religious life. They believe that the true
test of faith takes place on the plane of human relations. For Rosenzweig,
the individual is directed, that is, given the responsibility, to move from
the orbit of revelation, the dialogue of "I" and "Thou" with the divine,
to the orbit of redemption, the exchange of "I" and "Thou" between persons. It is in this way that God's work of redemption is brought to fruition.
Somewhat differently, with Buber the dialogue of I and Thou with other
persons actually precedes the relationship to God. That first exchange is
the training or discipline that leads to the dialogue with the eternal Thou.

Most importantly in the context of the present discussion, Rosenzweig
and Buber insist that the commandment to love the neighbor is not exclusive to one's religious community. The neighbor is precisely the *nebenmensch*
(the next one), that is, every other who is placed before the individual in the
midst of life. The inclusiveness of this relationship to the other, rendered

by Rosenzweig as loving the neighbor, by Buber in terms of the I and Thou encounter, and by Emmanuel Levinas as the face-to-face relation, is affirmed by the contemporary philosopher Hilary Putnam. In discussing the understanding of Levinas and Rosenzweig, which equally pertains to Buber, he writes, "Levinas ... believes that meaningful love of the other, the love that makes one ... 'a human being worthy of the name,' cannot be selective love. ... I have to be able to love each and every human being as a human being" (2008, 48–49).

Finally, beyond these issues, I want to offer a further reflection on Benjamin's essential insistence on the responsibility for witnessing the suffering of others. Such witnessing is demanded despite the individual's lack of responsibility for any decision or action that caused the victim's suffering. She even intimates that the failure to authentically respond to this situation for which one is innocent in the context of ethical theory, legal proceedings, and "common sense," i.e., everyday discourse, can itself be seen as an act of violence. In her words, "bystanders appear—at least in the victim's mind—as virtually the same as perpetrators" (2014c).

The standpoint that one is responsible even for acts by others, and that the failure to respond is itself a moral failure, is the signature position of Levinas. For him, subjectivity, the authentic subject, is not a thing, it is a project or way of living. It cannot be accomplished by the self itself. It is a way of responding to a calling from another human being. The calling is always already there and metaphorically seen in the face of the other; "I understand responsibility as responsibility for the Other, thus as responsibility for what is not my deed. ... [It] is met by me as face" (1985, 95).

The religious foundation for this portrait of true humanity is expressed by Levinas in a variety of ways. For him, it comes from a trace of the divine behind the face of the other, or it is seen through "the first word of the face [in the commandment] 'Thou shalt not kill'" (1985, 89), or it embodies the very definition of being a creature, or it constitutes the resounding message of the biblical stories of Job and Jonah. In terms of the latter, he writes of this "unlimited initial responsibility" for the neighbor, "The impossibility of escaping God, the adventure of Jonas ... lies in the depths of myself as a self," which is nothing less than "the birth of a meaning in the obtuseness of being" (1981, 128).[6]

In all, for the Jewish philosophers discussed here, faith is a matter of trust, of risk and not certainty, in the abiding presence of that "absolute" person. The unremitting temptation to affirm the "*Gott mit uns*" of exclusivism discovers its indomitable foe in that obligation to love the concrete other, and thus all possible others, encountered in the midst of life.

Notes

1   Rosenzweig's view of history as the story of war and revolution is examined in Alexander Altmann's essay "Franz Rosenzweig on History" in Mendes-Flohr 1988, 124–137.

2 See the author's essay "Can We Still Stay with Him?: Two Jewish Theologians Confront the Holocaust (Emil Fackenheim and Arthur Cohen)" in Oppenheim 2009, 273–298.

3 See note 2 as well as the author's essay "Rosenzweig and Levinas: On Anthropomorphism, the Holocaust, and God's Presence" in Oppenheim 1997, 28–52.

4 Levinas metaphorically uses the term "trauma" to underscore the point that this giving over to the welfare of the other comes as a shock to the self and self-interest. He describes this as a persecution, as being held hostage to the ethical call of the other. In Levinas' words, "This trauma ... takes shape as a subjection to the neighbor" (1996, 142).

5 This view of religious language is not restricted to these Jewish philosophers. In his most philosophical text, through the voice of the pseudonym Johannes Climacus, Søren Kierkegaard writes,

> *An objective uncertainty held fast in an appropriation-process of the most passionate inwardness is the truth,* the highest truth attainable for an *existing* individual. ... Without risk there is no faith. Faith is precisely the contradiction between the infinite passion of the individual's inwardness and the objective [scientific or philosophical] uncertainty.

> (1968, 182)

Dietrich Bonhoeffer writes, in his *Letters and Papers from Prison,*

> It just isn't true to say that Christianity alone ... has the answers [to such problems as "guilt, suffering and death"]. In fact the Christian answers are not more conclusive or compelling than any of the others.

> (1959, 142–143)

6 In *Doer and Done To* Benjamin offers a critique of Levinas' stance that the ethical approach to the other arises out of a shattering demand from the face. Characteristically, she insists on the primacy of identification in the response to the vulnerable other, writing, "Remorse and recognition of our wishes to escape both the painful identification with vulnerability and the hateful projection of it into the Other seems to be a starting point for a psychoanalytically informed ethics of a world where more than one can live" (2018, 245). It can be suggested that the divine-human relationship in the thought of the Jewish philosophers plays a similar role to that of the processes of identification in Benjamin's oeuvre. For Benjamin identification uncovers the basic vulnerability and moral unreliability of each person, while for the Jewish philosophers the God-relationship underscores the sense of dependency, humility, and limited or precarious moral accountability.

5 Two discourses
Distinctive approaches, intriguing correlations

This chapter features areas of comparison and correlation between the two discourses, contemporary psychology and modern Jewish philosophy. This approach reinforces the insights emerging from the discourses, as well as adding new dimensions to similar ideas. The specific topics discussed in the preceding chapters again order the material, although, as will become obvious, they are significantly intertwined and some themes will reappear within different contexts.

The guiding postulate of this investigation has been that the exploration of basic trust heightens the understanding of trauma, and that through the examination of trauma, features of basic trust will come to be seen in a new light. A major consequence of this dynamic concerns the enhanced appreciation for the role of the intersubjective in human life. Parallel streams within the two discourses provide both the material and the perspectives. The discourses feature the judgment that basic trust or trust in God is fundamental to living and that without it life cannot go on, since it grounds a plethora of essential elements, including the relationships to self, others, and world, as well as the features of hope and meaning. Within both there is the shared understanding that despite the importance of trust, it is not immutable. Trauma is its dissolution, and while the effects of trauma, at a minimum, leave traces, some range of recovery is still possible.

The literature on trauma is filled with discussion of its inner dialectic, between such features as knowing and not knowing, past and present, and hyper-arousal and passivity. The notion of dialectic, opposition within entwined relation, like syntonic and dystonic, is equally relevant to the pairing of trust and trauma. The dialectic of dissociation and fragmentation wreaked upon the traumatized self is the reverse image of the processes or binding force of trust. One learns from this that trust is not just the basis and foundation of the self, but the very glue that binds self and others together. This holds also for the Jewish philosophical discourse, where *emunah* is consistently and correctly translated as trust (in God).

The issue of the genesis of basic trust—"the most fundamental prerequisite of mental vitality" (Erikson 1968, 96)—is clear in the first discourse, originating within the mother–infant dyad through the mother's loving approach and reliable responses. As the severe phenomenon of developmental trauma indicates, bereft of the crucial dyadic experience, through absence or abuse, the path toward cultivating this primary psychosocial strength is perilous. The issue of the genesis of trust in God is not directly addressed by the Jewish philosophers examined in this inquiry. In brief, they may share an attitude that the trust emerges in the course of life, in a distinct revelation or through a developing sense of God's presence. Their concern is more pointed toward the ways that trust is lived out and verified in the midst of life, as exemplified in the concluding words of Rosenzweig's *Star*—"into life"—and Buber's admonition, "The meaning we receive [in Revelation] can be put to the proof in action only by each person in the uniqueness of his being and in the uniqueness of his life" (1970, 159).

There is an important synergy between the two discourses on the topic of hope. Erikson viewed hope as the psychosocial virtue corresponding to trust, and wrote, "Hope connotes the most basic quality of 'I'-ness, without which life could not begin or meaningfully end" (1997, 62). Seen from the other side of the dynamic, the haunting hopelessness and powerlessness of the victims of trauma is noted in many psychological reports. Rosenzweig and Heschel tied trust and hope together, the latter in terms of the messianic coming. In the wake of the Holocaust, while no resolution or justification was expected or even desired, the Jewish philosophers still held out the hope for a return of the dialogue between heaven and earth, regardless of what form God's presence might take. This analysis also suggests a recurring theme, that trust in God is not a matter of certainty. Actually, the word trust, regardless of the context, never connotes certainty. Trust is based on prior experience and it implies an attitude—what Heschel termed an "expectation" (1974, 290)—toward something in the future or at least something not fully realized in the present.

The earlier suggestion in Chapter 2 of the syntonic and dystonic pairing of trust and despair in the lexicon of the psychologists also makes sense in the context of the philosophers' discourse. Just as the term "belief" fails to have the resonance in their work that "trust" does, the full impact of the challenge of the Holocaust cannot be intellectually or experientially captured by the terms "unbelief" or "doubt." The Holocaust threatens the trust in God with the despairing emptiness of hope and meaning. The powerful protests of Wiesel and Levinas to the "empty sky" underscore this lesson.

The connection between trust and meaning is affirmed in both discourses. For the psychologists, meaning is seen in terms of the world order, what Benjamin terms "a larger principle of necessity, rightness, goodness" (2007, 9), and even more often in the context of human relations—Van der Kolk's "Safe connections are fundamental to meaningful and satisfying lives" (2015, 81). Heschel's statement, "God and meaning, as we understand them, are one" (1974, 290) is also representative of the other Jewish philosophers. Trauma undermines this necessity of human life, its effects seen by Herman in terms of " 'shattered assumptions' about meaning, order, and justice in the world" (2015, 178). Elie Wiesel's lament concerning the Holocaust stands on its own; for him, it signified the "defeat of the intellect that wants to find a Meaning—with a capital *M*—in history" (2000, 71). In this light, a key feature of psychological repair is seen as the restoration of trust in the possibility of a meaningful life and the belief in some type of wider lawfulness or moral dimension. For the Jewish philosophers, all that is left in the Holocaust's wake is the prospect of a future divine presence, but one that is unable to explain or atone for what occurred. A sense of this feeling of being adrift is caught in Buber's statement, "Today I no longer know exactly what Jewish life is" (2003a, 173).

One corollary of the Jewish philosophers' discussion of the trust in God extends to language or speech. Rosenzweig writes that the word of God and the word of humans are the same. Buber sees trust in God as the foundation for the "unreserved intercourse with the other" (1999, 201). In all, there are two dimensions to this trust in language or speech. One is that words themselves, or language, are adequate to express and communicate the full range of human feelings and experience. Rosenzweig contrasts René Descartes' famous *cogito ergo sum*, "I think therefore I am," with his own motto, "The best things you can tell" (quoted in Rosenstock-Huessy 1971, 163). He frequently disputes the view that words are insufficient, and that the individual is thus abandoned as an essentially walled-off solitary being. The second feature of trust in language, or speech, concerns the significance that is attached to dialogue or conversation. Both Rosenzweig and Buber are champions of dialogue. Rosenzweig characterizes his philosophical method as "speech-thinking," which celebrates the power of conversation to elicit both truth and the new (1999a, 86–87). Buber is renowned for his notion of the "life of dialogue" as the essential "turning towards the other" (1965, 22). However, the experience of the Holocaust attacks this trust in language, especially as its victims and commentators continually address the inability of language to cope with its trauma. Wiesel notes that the survivors "could never express in words, coherent, intelligible words, our experience of madness on an absolute scale" (1979, 201). He and others persistently plumb the notion of silence to portray the unfathomability of the Holocaust.

The literature of the psychologists also highlights the lack of the power of words to encompass either the victim's traumatic experiences or their aftereffects. Trauma is the "unspeakable" (Herman 2015, 1)—"moments of terror that they [survivors] cannot describe in words" (239). While great attention is paid to the singular importance of the excruciating, halting dialogic work in therapy, there does not seem to be a sufficient appreciation for the prior trust in language, particularly its power to express and communicate with others in the vast majority of life-situations. However, in the clinical context, Orange's "hermeneutics of trust" (2011, 31–35) contours a sensitive, trusting listening to patients that finds in their words an effort to relate and to communicate: "Above all, we trust the other to teach us. As psychoanalysts, we rely on the patient to teach us about her or his suffering, we search for meaning—both found and created—together" (206).

The topic of narrative is interlaced with the prior discussions of meaning and language. Narrative or story features the report or even unexpressed understanding of an experience or experiences within a space-time orientation, that is, of connected events with some sense of a beginning, development, and conclusion. Erikson's basic trust includes the view that the interaction with the mother initiates the infant's sense of temporality, causation, and the differentiations between inside and outside, and self and others. Trauma, particularly the oftentimes accompanying feature of dissociation, undermines these orientations; in Herman's words, "intense sensory and emotional experiences are disconnected from the social domain of language and memory" (2015, 239). As we have seen, a key feature of therapy is to help the patient produce a narrative account of the traumatic experience(s) in terms of time, place, events, persons, and the wider context of the individual's life.

Rosenzweig can be seen to address the issue of narrative, in the sense of an overall historical orientation of the individual and the religious community. For him, the direct, personal relationship to God opens the panorama of categories: Creation, Revelation, and Redemption. The basic understanding expressed through these orienting categories allows the individual to live out everyday life with purpose. This is the message of his condensed version of the *Star*, *Understanding the Sick and the Healthy*, as well as the more developed texts. Rosenzweig concludes, "To avail himself of today, man must, for better or worse, put his trust in God" (1999b, 93).

The topic of narrative or *midrash* is also prominent in Wiesel's and Fackenheim's reflections on the Holocaust. They insist that no ordered story can explain or justify the horror on an absolute scale of this trauma, since it undermines the relationship to God as well as such concomitant trusts in language, meaning, and hope. Especially for Wiesel, this is the in-between of terror and promise, in which only madness and silence reign.

Stolorow's notion of the "absolutisms of everyday life," "that allow one to function in the world, experienced as stable and predictable" (2007, 16), presents a condensed psychological overview of trust in the world. However, his personal experience of tragedy overturned this platform of stability and predictability.[1] He was brought to understand that the "absolutisms" were merely a veneer covering the chaos that may erupt at any time and the finitude that haunts all the living. For the Jewish philosophers, the trust in God could be viewed similarly, but certainly not as a veneer. The concept of Creation, the world as created, entails that life is, in essence, both meaningful and good. While trauma can challenge this perspective, there is no life, at least life with integrity and meaning, without this trust. In consequence, the Jewish philosophers can be seen to vigorously reject the position that this feature is merely naïve or illusory.

It is important to note that for the psychologists and philosophers, a sense of agency is fundamental to basic trust. Life is not meant to be lived in mere contemplation, but in action with and for others. For example, Rosenzweig disparages the mystic, who "is only the vessel of the raptures he feels," as "scarcely half a man," because "his life is only waiting and not walking forward" (2005, 224). An element of responsibility for others is emphatically expressed in Benjamin's notion that in the wake of traumatic episodes, there is an imperative for others to witness those injured and to affirm both the unity of the human community and the inviolability of justice (2018, 216). The philosophers' understanding of the command to love the neighbor, especially Levinas' view of the absolute responsibility for the other, also powerfully affirms this idea. In both discourses, humans have a responsibility to witness and reinforce the meaning and justice woven into existence.

Intersubjectivity

Intersubjectivity is not just a recurrent topic in the examination of trust and trauma, but a foundational theme that pervades the whole treatment. It provides the framework for the psychological understanding of the nature of and dynamics between trust and trauma, the processes of repair, and the particular elements of self, others, and world. The intersubjective perspective is similarly reflected in the discourse of the Jewish philosophers through the abiding notion of God as person and the importance of dialogue.

For Erikson, basic trust is the preeminent fruit of the mother-infant dyad, continuing to impact and develop throughout all the following psychosocial stages. For Rosenzweig, trust in God is initiated through the individual's personal experience of God's turning toward them, and it provides the orientation and ground to step firmly into life. Erikson's reference to trust—"Trust … is here [in the dictionary] defined as 'the assured reliance on another's integrity'" (1963, 269)—and Rosenzweig's description of humility—"conscious of being what it is through the grace of a Higher Being" (2005, 181)—deeply mirror each other. Not surprisingly, Rosenzweig's concluding statement in the *Star* could equally apply, absent the religious reference, to Erikson's view of basic trust that is generated through relationships:

> To walk humbly with ~~your God~~ [others]—nothing more is asked for here than a wholly present trust. But trust is a great word. It is the seed from which faith, hope and love grow. … To walk humbly with ~~your God~~ [others]—the words are above the gate, the gate that leads … into life.
>
> (2005, 447)

The presence of the other as sympathetic and supporting or as disavowing and rejecting is a major factor, if not the major factor, in terms of the genesis and intensity of trauma. Stolorow's cryptic statement, "Pain is not pathology" (2007, 10), is expanded in Van der Kolk's judgment, "The critical issue is *reciprocity*: being heard and seen by the people around us, feeling that we are held in someone else's mind and heart" (2015, 81). All the psychological investigations echo the early finding of Ferenczi of the devastating effect of silence and rejection by others, particularly in the case of developmental trauma (1988, 193). In relation to the trauma of the Holocaust, the title of Wiesel's first book, *And the World Stayed Silent* (in Yiddish, 1956), starkly echoes this message concerning the devastating pain inflicted by those who refused to listen to the victims' cries. The silence of the world as the facts of the murder of millions of Jews became known was harder for Wiesel and other survivors to bear than the horrifying events themselves. As he writes, "At the risk of offending, it must be emphasized that the victims suffered more, and more profoundly, from the indifference of the onlookers than from the brutality of the executioner" (Morgan 1987, 72).

The process of recovery again points to the crucial significance of empathic support. The therapist must communicate trust, concern, and hope despite tremendous obstacles: facing suspicion and rejection, acknowledging moments of failure and despair, the requirement to "know terrible things," and accepting the responsibility to evoke devastating memories. Van der Kolk describes the help required of family, support groups, loved ones, and the wider community: "The role of those relationships is to provide physical and emotional safety, including safety from feeling shamed, admonished, or judged, and to bolster the courage to tolerate, face, and process the reality of what has happened" (2015, 212).

The Jewish philosophers can be seen to suggest that the reconstituted trust in God after the Holocaust has some similarities to the description of the path of therapeutic recovery. It is lengthy, no outcome is certain, and the lingering impact of the trauma cannot be completely escaped. The help of other victims and members of the religious community can be decisive, and beyond that it is a question of struggling to hear what Buber and Wiesel envision as a voice within the divine silence.

Trust in the self, others, and the world lucidly exhibits intersubjective features. As we have seen, a sense of the self's goodness, integrity, even self-love and self-respect, arise out of the mother-infant relation for the psychologists and the relationship to God in the view of the Jewish philosophers. As examples, Erikson sees this development through the lens of hope, trust's primary virtue: "The shortest formulation of the identity gain of earliest childhood may well be: I am what hope I have and give" (1968, 106–107). For Rosenzweig, the message that we are "dependent on the other for what is ours" echoes within the phenomenon of speech (1999a, 87). The intersubjective theme courses through both sides of relationships. What Erikson sees as "mutual activation" (1963, 165), and Herman as "a mutually enhancing interaction" (2015, 216), Rosenzweig offers as the power of speech and Buber regards as the gift of the I and Thou relation: "I require a Thou to become; becoming I, I say Thou" (1970, 62).

The topic of meaning illustrates one approach to understanding the significance of intersubjectivity in relation to the world. It is important to both basic trust and to recovery that there is a sense that life has meaning. This point can be made through the example of developmental trauma. Benjamin refers to an insight of the Object Relations theorist W. R. D. Fairbairn that "it is better for the child to feel that he is 'a sinner in a world ruled by God than to live in a world ruled by the Devil'" (Benjamin 2018, 229). This quote underscores the necessity that life exhibits some degree of both justice and meaning. The child is forced to turn upon themself with the accusation of sinner, rather than to concede that life is irredeemably permeated with injustice and meaninglessness, metaphorically expressed as "ruled by the Devil." However, the statement also reveals the import of the child's relationship to the primary caregiver. The child would rather see themself as guilty than condemn the caregiver as evil, and thus give up any hope for a positive relationship to that indispensable other. In Buber's *I and Thou*, meaning is given a central role in the description of the relationship or "association" with what may be termed the primary caregiver, God. In his words, "Nor does association make life any easier for us—it makes life heavier but heavy with meaning. ... Nothing, nothing can henceforth be meaningless. The question about the meaning of life has vanished" (1970, 158–159). Of course, as we have seen, Buber's later encounter with the Holocaust deeply threatened this "confirmation of meaning" (158).

The intersubjective dimension, which courses through the Jewish philosophical discourse about trust, trauma, and repair, is grounded in the metaphor of God as a person.

> The designation of God as a person is indispensable for all who, like myself ... mean by "God" him that, whatever else he may be in addition, enters into a direct relationship to us human beings through creative, revelatory, and redemptive acts, and thus makes it possible for us to enter into direct relationship to him. This ground and meaning of our existence establishes each time a mutuality of the kind that can obtain only between persons. ... From this last attribute I should then derive my own and all men's being persons.
>
> (Buber 1970, 180–181)

> The assumption they [biblical anthropomorphisms] make is ... that God is capable of what he wills (thus even of meeting the creature from time to time in fully bodily and spiritual reality) and that the creature is capable of what he should be (thus even of fully understanding and recognizing God's self-embodying or self-spiritualization from time to time turning toward him).
>
> (Rosenzweig 1998, 144)

The ability of this anthropomorphic metaphor to carry traumatized persons through the unprecedented trials of the Holocaust has often been portrayed, here in terms of the love of God:

> No one truly understands the meaning of love, nor does one even know whether he is in love, except through affliction.
>
> (Heschel 2007, 135)

> What happens to us touches God. What happens to Him concerns us. We share in the same adventure and participate in the same quest. We suffer for the same reasons and ascribe the same coefficient to our common hope.
>
> (Wiesel 1995, 103–104)

Dependency and vulnerability

Both trust and trauma feature dependency and vulnerability. Noted earlier was Erikson's reference to trust, "the assured reliance on another's integrity" (1963, 269), and Rosenzweig's parallel description of humility, "conscious of being what it is through the grace of a Higher Being" (2005, 181). Embedded within the psychoanalytic and Jewish philosophical discourses is the underlying insight that to be oneself in both a basic and authentic sense is a gift from another. For Rosenzweig, the very nature of the self entails that we are "dependent on the other for what is ours" (1999, 87). The finely researched essay by the psychoanalyst Susan Coates, "Having a Mind of One's Own and Holding the Other in Mind," supplements Erikson's view of the significance of early trust by detailing how a child must "find his or her mind in the mind of the mother" in order to gain "a personalized, authentic, vitalized sense of self" (2005, 289). The feature of dependency clearly appears in the genealogy and treatment of trauma, as researchers have found that the nature of the response of others—whether of confirmation and support or denial and opposition—is the crucial factor in both regards.

The notion of vulnerability is underscored in a variety of ways. It obviously stems from the origins of trust in this reliance on the other, as well as from the lessons conveyed by trauma. Just as the literal self is formed through the early caregiver's responsive and loving attention to the infant, cases of neglect and abuse reveal the psychological vulnerability of the very young. Trauma's terrifying reach extends to all the stages and ages of the individual's life, which is part of the justification for Stolorow's assertion, once again, that trauma reveals itself as "a fundamental constituent of our existential constitution" (2007, 48).

An awareness of the possible collision with traumatic experience, actually even with the preponderance of everyday experience, goes to the heart of the vulnerability of religious trust. This acknowledgment is clearly articulated in Buber's interpretation of *emunah*, which pivots on the words "in spite": "By its very nature trust is substantiation of trust in the fullness of life in spite of the course of the world which is experienced" (2003b, 40). Buber offers the expectation that what may be the emptiness, amorality, or even violence within mundane experience, or at least its preponderant character, will directly conflict with trust in life's fullness or ultimate meaning. In the face of this torrent of the everyday, authentic religious trust is tested in order to remain steadfast. In an otherwise measured and circumspect treatment of the vast phenomenon of religious experience, James underscores this point: "If any one phrase could gather its [religion's] universal message, that phrase would be, 'All is *not* vanity in this Universe, whatever the appearances may suggest'" (2004, 29). Substituting "whatever" for Buber's "in spite," James recognizes that the tension between religious trust and events ("appearances") that may erupt at any moment is almost the very essence of religious consciousness.

The trauma of the Holocaust has added exponentially to our awareness of the vulnerability of trust in God to the vagaries of history. In *Quest for Past and Future*, Emil Fackenheim sketches out the degrees of Judaism's responses to history's challenges:

> In its historic career [Judaism] is able simply to absorb some novel events and experiences, is forced to respond to others through an internal restructuring and—this must be considered at least possible— is vulnerable to experiences so radical that the strain may be intolerable.
>
> (1968, 14)

The passionate struggles of Heschel and Buber, described in Chapter 3, represent just a small portion of the expansive philosophical and theological literature about the degree of the Holocaust's "strain" on faith/trust in God.

Dependency and vulnerability are today, in much of the Western world, often portrayed as negative qualities. However, this judgment is contingent on how human development, wellbeing, and authenticity are understood. Especially when autonomy and autarchy, that is, self-consciousness, self-reliance, and self-direction, are elevated to supreme values, are dependency and vulnerability seen in this way. A number of overlapping psychological and philosophical perspectives have challenged this understanding. For decades, feminist philosophers and psychoanalysts have detailed the ideological and psychological dynamics behind this elevation of human autonomy, focusing on the underlying patriarchal character of Western culture. For example, elements of the masculine myth of self-sufficiency and the projection of dependency, vulnerability, and permeability onto "the feminine" are exposed in the French feminist Luce Irigaray's masterful mimicry of Freud's sexual theory in her *Speculum of the Other Woman*, concluding with the section "Woman is a Woman as a Result of a Certain Lack of Characteristics" (1985, 112).

A number of psychoanalytic streams' re-evaluations of dependency and vulnerability arise out of the primary understanding of the intersubjective or interpersonal character of human life, that persons are born, develop, and mature through relationships with others. In the highly lauded work *Precarious Life*, Judith Butler writes, "We were never simply ourselves but were always part of others. ... Our common corporeal vulnerability is the very condition of our relationality, our very ability to love more than ourselves" (2006, 92). The "ethical turn" in philosophy and psychoanalysis also reflects this reconsideration (Goodman and Severson 2016, 1–18). Lewis Aron, in his essay "Mutual Vulnerability: An Ethic of Clinical Practice," writes,

> There is a significant trend among philosophers to ground the philosophy of ethics in the experience of vulnerability. ... I am suggesting that the ethos of psychoanalysis be rooted not in neutrality and objectivity, but rather in our acceptance and acknowledgment of mutual vulnerability.
>
> (2016, 24)

The work of Emmanuel Levinas and Jessica Benjamin can be seen as both embodying and influencing these perspectives. For them, accepting the vulnerability of both the self and the other plays a central role in the constitution of the ethical relationship. In Levinas' understanding of this relationship, the vulnerability of the self is expressed in terms of a radical openness to, of being taken hostage by, the inescapable ethical demand of the other. Yet, the persecuting demand from the other's height reveals at the same time their existential vulnerability to the self's natural will to a threatening, violent perseverance. Put in other words, the other's height expresses a transcendent ethical dimension, but on the everyday plane, where the *conatus essendi* rules, the other is the vulnerable stranger, poor, orphan, and widow. Levinas writes, "The transcendence of the Other, which is his eminence, his height, his lordship, in its concrete meaning includes his destitution, his exile, and his rights as a stranger" (1969, 76–77). Benjamin envisions the self's sense of vulnerability coming into play in confronting the ethical responsibility to witness the traumatic suffering of the other. The failed witness embraces the notion of the self's innocence and inviolability in order to avoid identifying and empathizing with that other. This posture condemns the other as alien, guilty, and deserving of their plight. Recognition of the common vulnerability and dignity of all persons, as well as the responsibility to witness the ideal of a just world, are core features of Benjamin's "moral third," of "a psychoanalytically informed ethics of a world where more than one can live" (2018, 245).

Still, the qualities of dependency and vulnerability do not exhaust the mechanisms that underlie trust. There is a startling panorama of perspectives detailing the mutuality, as well as asymmetry,[2] manifest in the articulation of trust. Erikson's notion of *"mutual activation"* is a fundamental tenet that runs through all his psychosocial stages, "a network of mutual influences within which the person actuates others even as he is actuated, and within which the person is 'inspired with active properties,' even as he so inspires others" (1964, 165). Judith Herman's description of "mutually enhancing interaction" duplicates Erikson's insight: "As each participant extends herself to others she becomes more capable of receiving the gifts that others have to offer. The tolerance, compassion and love she grants to others begin to rebound upon herself" (2015, 215–216). Benjamin's signature concept of recognition, that is, the treatment of and respect for the other as a person in their own right, highlighting such features as their intentionality and agency, echoes this interchange: "We have a need for recognition and … we have a capacity to recognize others in return, thus making mutual recognition possible" (1995, 30). Even Levinas' notion of the asymmetrical relationship of the self's radical responsibility for the other has consequences for both sides of the encounter. As Donna Orange explains, "This radical passivity, vulnerability, or receptivity [to the other] we might rename the ethical formation of [the self's] subjectivity" (2016, 5–6).

Mutuality is a pervasive feature of the way Rosenzweig and Buber, the two Jewish philosophers of dialogue, characterize both the authentic relationship between humans and the encounter with the divine. In Rosenzweig's account of speech, "it does not know beforehand where it will emerge; it lets itself be given its cues from others; it actually lives by another's life" (1999a, 86). Buber's characterization of the I–Thou relationship is summarized as: "Relation is reciprocity. My Thou acts on me and I act on it" (1970, 67). Further, while the mutuality of the relationship between the human and the divine is scandalous in some religious quarters, Rosenzweig and Buber attest to this understanding in their most important works. In *The Star of Redemption*, Rosenzweig refers to a mystical interpretation of *Isaiah* 43:12: "If you testify to me, then I shall be God, and otherwise not" (2005, 185). Buber writes in *I and Thou*, "You need God in order to be, and God needs you—for that which is the meaning of your life" (1970, 130), and ends his 1957 addendum with the message, "Anyone who dares nevertheless to speak of it ['the existence of mutuality between God and man'] bears witness and invokes the witness of those whom he addresses—present or future witnesses" (182).[3]

An existential symmetry

The conclusion of Chapter 2 noted the correspondence between what Erikson terms "basic trust" and crucial conceptions of four psychologists: Stolorow's "absolutisms of everyday life," Benjamin's cornerstone "moral third," and Herman's and Van der Kolk's view of safety. A principal insight of the present chapter extends the parallel to what the Jewish philosophers describe as trust in God. Throughout this treatment, the

Jewish philosophers' understanding of faith/trust has been juxtaposed with Erikson's concept of trust. The similarities are especially pronounced in terms of trust's compass of self, others, and world and the allied topic of hope. What Stolorow adds to this configuration is that for the psychologists and philosophers, basic trust is taken for granted, that is, it is so integrated into everyday experience that it is almost unnoticed. However, Stolorow also found that trust is deeply vulnerable to trauma, leaving the individual naked to the ravages of alienation and despair.

Using a different vocabulary and set of narratives, the Jewish philosophers forcefully express parallel ideas to the central principles of Benjamin's moral third. Trust or belief in a universal "lawfulness" is enunciated in terms of a trust or faith in the divine moral order or design. The dignity of all persons, the individual's responsibility for others, and the inclusiveness or union of the human community are powerfully detailed in terms of the inescapable commandment to "love the neighbor," to embark on a life of "I and Thou," and to harken to the moral demand of "the face." All humans are brought together as one's neighbors, as partners or "Thous" to one's "I," or as what Levinas designates as the "fraternity" of all persons (1987, 123).[4]

Lastly, the concept of safety utilized by Herman and Van der Kolk can be seen to supplement the force of the "absolutisms," and the "moral third." The absolutisms function as a safety net, a sense of solidness and permanence to everyday life, while the moral third provides an additional sense that, despite some conflicting experiences, the world manifests a moral order. Clearly, as exhibited in Psalm 23, safety is the paramount feeling that God's presence provides even while traversing "through the valley of the shadow of death." In Rosenzweig's words, "It [the transformed self] knows that nothing can happen to it" (2005, 181). The psychologists and the Jewish philosophers conclude that without these dimensions of trust, paraphrasing the words of Erikson, life just cannot go on in any worthwhile sense.

Notes

1 Stolorow was devastated by the precipitous death of his young wife (2007, 41).
2 Lewis Aron's *A Meeting of Minds: Mutuality in Psychoanalysis* features the dynamic relationship between mutuality and asymmetry (1996, 98–100).
3 Aron expresses in very personal terms the relationship he sees between his "psychoanalytic vision" and his "religious ethos":

> Mutual vulnerability is a concept at the heart of the particular Jewish philosophy that inspires me. Abraham Joshua Heschel ... suggested that we have to understand the prophetic God as a God of pathos, a feelingful God who cares about the world and about people.

(2016, 35)

4 I am suggesting another perspective on Jessica Benjamin's important work concerning witnessing, acknowledging, and repair. This follows the critique of

the abstract language of the moral third detailed in Chapter 1. I am not pro-posing that religious language should be substituted for her psychoanalytic dis-course, only that the Jewish philosophers discussed here offer an approach that is possibly more compelling to and in harmony with the life-worlds of many religious witnesses, victims, and perpetrators. It is not incumbent upon Benjamin to employ these religious ideas, but a path is open to other theorists to make her insights more accessible.

Conclusion

An interdisciplinary study in human nature

This concluding section introduces three new optics to deepen and widen the investigation of *Trust and Trauma*: William James' position that the exploration of religious experiences is an appropriate entrée to understanding "human nature"; Steven Mitchell's intricate diagram of an "interactional hierarchy" of relationality; and D. W. Winnicott's paradoxical reflection on what it takes to "be alone."

The study of trust and trauma is more than an investigation into two interesting and enigmatic psychological features of the mind, or even opposing elements of religious consciousness. The examination of these topics opens to nothing less than what the psychologist William James offers through his 1901–1902 lectures on *The Varieties of Religious Experience*, which he subtitles "a study in human nature" (2004, iii).[1] The contention that basic trust lies at the foundation of human living and experience is expressed in a variety of ways. Erik Erikson speaks of it as "the most fundamental prerequisite of mental vitality" (1968, 96), while Robert Stolorow holds that the correlate "absolutisms of everyday life" constitute that "naive realism and optimism that allow one to function in the world, experienced as stable and predictable" (2007, 16). Jessica Benjamin argues that the "sense of the *lawful world*," which comprises the core of her "moral third," is nothing less than "a central category of experience" (2018, 6). The Jewish philosophers are equally adamant about the ramifications of faith/trust in God. Abraham Joshua Heschel writes, "Expectation of meaning is an *a priori* condition of our existence," and "God and meaning, as we understand them, are one" (1974, 290). Martin Buber can be seen to add that "our faith has our humanity as its foundation, and our humanity has our faith as its foundation" (1999, 117), a proposition that Franz Rosenzweig echoes in his simple statement that trust in God leads "into life" (2005, 447).

The impact of traumatic experience upon human living is equally comprehensive. Judith Herman contends that "traumatized people suffer damage to the basic structures of the self" (2015, 56), and Stolorow elevates the lessons of emotional trauma to the degree that they are "a fundamental constituent of our existential constitution" (2015, 48). In reflecting on the trauma of the Holocaust, Elie Wiesel writes that "in truth, Auschwitz signifies ... the defeat of the intellect that wants to find a Meaning—with a capital *M*—in history" (2000, 71), and Emil Fackenheim concludes, "But the Holocaust calls into question not this or that way of being human, but *all* ways" (1982, 262).

In all, this line of inquiry leads to the exploration of many of the most significant elements of vital human living: hope, faith, meaning, and responsibility. Equally, the darker side of mistrust, isolation, and despair is not ignored. Trust and trauma are almost mirror images of each other, or perhaps trauma resembles the photographic negative that produces the full picture. Hope, meaning, significant human contacts, and other attributes of trust are precisely what are attacked, with such devastation, by trauma.

Axes of intersubjectivity

Stephen Mitchell, in the chapter "An Interactional Hierarchy" of *Relationality* (2000), elaborates four modes or axes of the individual's life with others, "both our relational embeddedness with others (in the interpersonal field) and the embeddedness of others within our own minds (in the internal world)" (69).[2] How does the examination of trust and trauma relate to this scheme? Does Mitchell's intricate detailing of unconscious and conscious exchanges illuminate the emergence and development of trust? Conversely, does the study of trust and trauma add new dimensions to Mitchell's arrangement?

Mitchell's presentation represents an attempt to bring together insights from a number of post-Freudian relational streams—among these are self-psychology, object relations theory, interpersonal psychoanalysis, and relational psychoanalysis—along with recent discoveries in the study of infant development. His four-stage "interactional hierarchy" includes dimensions of affect, behavior, and language in dynamic configurations. The four modes developmentally emerge sequentially, show increasing sophistication, and in adult life are always operative, although at any one time a particular axis will be more dominant than the others. Together they offer an excellent charting of various intrapsychic and interpersonal dimensions,[3] which are incorporated into Mitchell's overall view of human relationality.

The earliest form of interaction between infant and mother takes place below conscious awareness. This dimension of "non-reflective behavior" is constituted by the complex "choreography" of reciprocal actions through which the two partners impact each other in cycles of exchange (2000, 59). Discrete linkages of eye movements, facial expressions, and vocalizations, as well as the infant's instinctual actions of sucking and clinging, wind into cycles of initiation and response. In adult life these pre-symbolic patterns are seen in, and help constitute, intimate relationships between partners.

The second form, "affective permeability," points to the transpersonal and contagious features of human emotions (Mitchell 2000, 61). Powerful emotions such as terror, rage, fear, and love can effectively capture those engaged in intense relationships. The question of who has what emotion evaporates when, as one of Mitchell's patients expresses it, "love is in the air" (67). A good example of this affective phenomenon is illustrated in recent work on analytic interactions, in which the analyst sometimes reflects on her own litany of emotions as guides to both what the patient feels and to what is taking place between them.

"Self-other configurations" are patterns of interaction that are put in symbolic forms of "me" and "you," as in father–son, mother–daughter, and older to younger sibling (Mitchell 2000, 62). In terms of the former, Mitchell writes, "In each of these relationships, I have both shaped myself in relation to my parents and internalized a sense of my parents in relation to me" (62). For example, a particular feeling or feelings about the self, or sense of the self—such as confident or insecure, dependable or impulsive—might at times exist as a deep residual of the relationship with a specific significant other. Moreover, there would be a corresponding internalized sense of that other, as perhaps supportive or judgmental. These multiple symbolic patterns are carried both unconsciously and consciously, and forcefully illustrate the numerous discontinuous features of what is often seen as a single, harmonious self. For many relational psychoanalysts, these self-other configurations signify more than discrete features or facets of the self; they are each complete functional units (selves) or alternatively ecosystems, with their corresponding beliefs, feelings, purposes, and developmental history.

The last mode of relationality is "intersubjectivity," defined by Mitchell in a more narrow way than throughout this study, as the relations between persons "with self-reflective intentionality (thinking about and trying to do things) and dependency (upon other agents for completion)" (2000, 64). This primarily concerns the dynamic of being recognized as a full and unique subject by another person. Mitchell notes that particularly in the West, such recognition is regarded as both elemental and essential to human life. This understanding has had significant impact on theorizing about the analytic situation, which over the last decades has moved from Freud's basically subject–object model (the analyst as observer and interpreter) to a subject–subject model, or two-person analysis, where the dynamic respects the intentionality and dependency of the two partners in dialogue.[4]

In terms of the wider context of this investigation, Mitchell's four-stage hierarchy can be used to illustrate the discreet relational processes that establish trust, especially during the earliest psychosocial stages. The seeds of trust develop through the first type of interaction within the mother–infant dyad, that is, what Mitchell terms non-reflective behavior. Out of the synchronized attunement and exchange of subtle movements and sounds between the two subjects, an overall sense of rapport and reliability develops. The infant realizes that the m/other can be trusted to know and reliably respond to their requirements, and also that those felt needs are justified. The mother learns to trust her sense of the infant's needs and her ability to effectively react to these. Mitchell's "affective permeability" describes the overall climate of trust, attunement, and reliability that now envelops the dyad. The axis of "self–other configurations" explains the way each side of the dyad internalizes and stores these feelings—experiencing the self as trusting and confident and the other as loving and supportive. Finally, Mitchell's fourth axis, "intersubjectivity," is exemplified by Benjamin's concept of the "moral third," that is, of the mutually developing recognition of the independence and integrity of each person within this early dyad.

Since Mitchell's four axes are helpful in understanding the formation of trust, it is justifiable to surmise that they might also identify some of the processes that trauma undermines. Trauma's attack on intersubjectivity, resulting in overwhelming feelings of alienation and isolation, is one of its diagnostic features. In this instance, these feelings reflect the disruption or dissipation within ordinary and significant relationships of "non-reflective behavior" with its interpersonal micro-adaptations and cycles of cue and response, "affective permeability" with the sharing of powerful affects, "self-other configurations" of stored experiences and their lessons, and "intersubjectivity" with the sense of the dignity and integrity of self and others.

Mitchell's presentation of relational processes provides an especially interesting portal into Benjamin's treatment of a trauma patient, discussed in Chapter 1. Benjamin relates,

> I heard her [Jeannette] telling me that she needed me to embody *some* limit, some principle of right and wrong that I truly believed in, and that she could therefore believe in, too. This message from her was my first encounter in the context of violence with what I later came to formulate as the moral Third.
>
> (2018, 211)

The request by Jeannette, as well as Benjamin's response, are somewhat misleading, because they seem to place the requirement to embody or model some sense of justice—"principle of right and wrong"—on Benjamin as the therapeutic agent in the analytic relationship. However, as Mitchell's description of the dynamics within intimate dyads indicates, it is not one side or the other that has a responsibility, or even the ability, to create or "embody" something of this kind. The trust that some form of justice exists in this interpersonal microcosm as well as the wider world can only be embodied, that is emerge, through various processes performed within the dyad. It is the couple (intersubjective dimension) that succeeds or fails to embody justice, through the different behaviors and affects, which are then internalized (intrapsychic dimension) by each partner. This is an example of what Mitchell in a different situation described as an

> affective experience that could exist only if it operated in both of them, an experience that required two participants to ignite and fuel. … It is

not simply in either or both of them; it has a transpersonal quality and operates in the field that they comprise together.

(2000, 68)

Following Mitchell, it is obvious that the quality of justice is not simply in one or the other partner, but how is the statement that it is not in "both" accurate? The term "both" implies that a similar quality is somehow owned by each partner, but it is, more precisely, only in the context of the dyad— "in the field that they comprise together," either actually or in memory, consciously or unconsciously—that the quality exists. This episode also reveals how Mitchell's description of the four-stage interactional hierarchy helps in uncovering discrete processes behind the emergence of a sense of justice, one of the constituent qualities of basic trust.

Conversely, the exploration of basic trust can be seen to provide two significant supplementary features to Mitchell's original presentation. First, while the focal point of Mitchell's analysis is interactive *psychological processes*, the emphasis of Erikson's discussion of the first psychosocial stage is the *values and virtues* aligned with basic trust. These, along with the correlative insights of Herman, Van der Kolk, Stolorow, and Benjamin, reveal that the processes that Mitchell details may have specific *outcomes* that are the very basis of vital human living. In terms of the individual, these outcomes include: confidence, a sense of inner goodness, self-love, a feeling of safety, and the virtue that Erikson identifies as corresponding to trust, which is hope.

Second, through the alignment of basic trust with Mitchell's four "modes" of relationality, the latter can be seen to have effects that extend beyond the individual and even the specific relational partner. As detailed in Chapter 2, the scope of the values and virtues aligned with basic trust extends to the whole human community as well as to a vision of the wider world or cosmos. This suggests that the overall sense of safety, the feeling of being part of and responsible for the wider human community, and the expectation of some elementary justice and lawfulness in the world can be seen as outcomes of the processes Mitchell outlines.

Finally, the psychological approach to trust and especially Mitchell's relational hierarchy may also contribute to understanding some of the formative dynamics in Buber's portrayal of intersubjectivity through the I–Thou relationship. Buber's description of that relationship as mutual, reciprocal, exclusive, and timeless (1970, 63) at times appears quite abstract, especially in comparison with Mitchell's descriptions of the intricate behavioral and affective interactions through the four modes of relationality. In this context, Mitchell can be seen to provide an enlightening approach to the concrete—conscious and unconscious, intrapsychic and interpersonal— processes that underlie the exchange of "I" and "Thou."

Two examples of meetings between persons illustrate this suggestion. The importance of the first instance is highlighted in that Buber uses it as the first example in the effort "to clarify the 'dialogical' principle" presented *I and Thou* (1965, xi). He labels this episode "Silence which is communication":

> Imagine two men sitting beside one another in any kind of solitude of the world. They do not speak with one another. ... Unreservedly communication streams from him [one of the individuals], and the silence bears it to his neighbour. ... For where unreserve has ruled, even wordlessly, between men, the word of dialogue has happened sacramentally.
>
> (4)

Mitchell's axes may illuminate the mystery of this "dialogue." Not needing words, the two may communicate through: unconscious synchronized attunement and mirroring of subtle movements, an enveloping climate of trust that permeates the two persons, perhaps some transference in each of them from earlier significant relationships, or an exchange of respect embodied in glances.

The second example is taken from a real meeting or rather mismeeting. This is also an important episode in Buber's life that leads to the rejection of his earlier fascination with aestheticism and mysticism. In this case, ironically, friendly words are exchanged, but no "I and Thou" appears, and no trust or meaning is created. He writes, "I had a visit from an unknown young man, without being there in spirit. I certainly did not fail to let the meeting be friendly. ... I conversed attentively and openly with him" (1967a, 24). Here once again, Mitchell's presentation may help in giving concreteness to this not "being there in spirit." What may be missing are unconscious reciprocal actions, shared emotions, transference self-other connections, and mutual recognition of the other as a unique person. In this way, from the opposite poles of words and wordlessness, possible underlying psychological processes of the I–Thou relation are brought to light.

The personal God or God as a person

The religious idea of a personal God both draws upon and emphasizes the paramount role of intersubjectivity in the constitution of individual subjectivity, especially in relation to the "strength" of basic trust. A number of the psychologists and philosophers address these connections.

Erikson, appropriately, concentrates on the platform for the first psychosocial stage, the mother–infant dyad, and the vital feature of the face-to-face. He explicitly relates the enduring sweep of that primary interaction to the relationship with the personal God:

> Here we are again reminded of the lifelong power of the first mutual recognition of the newborn and the *primal* (maternal) *other* and its eventual transfer to the *ultimate other* who will "lift up His countenance upon you and give you peace."
>
> (1997, 88)

The importance of the image of God's countenance also is central to the conclusion of Rosenzweig's epic *Star*. He refers to the features of the human countenance, especially the eyes and mouth, that confirm the presence and support of the divine, adding, "In the innermost sanctuary of divine truth ... man beholds nothing other than a countenance like his own" (2005, 446).

Another perspective on the psychological pertinence of the notion of the personal God is seen in the object-relations psychoanalyst D. W. Winnicott's (1896–1971) influential essay "The Capacity to Be Alone" (1958). Since experiences within the mother–infant dyad comprise the beginning of the baby's existence, creating the very basis for the infant's subjective life, Winnicott asks how it is possible that an individual in later life can actually be alone. Mature being alone requires that the individual feel secure and be at peace, that is, not haunted by inner psychic doubts and conflicts, or by fears about the dangers of the outside environment. Winnicott's answer is that the relationship with the mother is what first allays these basic disturbances and fears, and that it is only by keeping the mother in mind as a supporting inner presence that these continue to be dispelled in later life.[5] His article concludes with the lines,

> Gradually, the ego-supportive environment [of the mother–infant dyad] is introjected and built into the individual's personality, so that there comes about a capacity actually to be alone. Even so, theoretically, there is always someone present, someone who is equated ultimately and unconsciously with the mother, the person who, in the early days and weeks, was temporarily identified with her infant, and for the time being was interested in nothing else but the care of her own infant.
>
> (420)

Although Winnicott does not use the term, he is describing what Erikson sees as the emergence and continuing relevance of basic trust. For Erikson, trust concerns a sense of assurance about the self, others, and the wider environment. Winnicott describes the mother's support in terms of feeling "a relative freedom from [inner] persecutory anxiety" (1958, 418), being "confident about the present and the future" (417), and "belief in a benign environment" (417). Additionally, this freedom and confidence are not just relevant to being alone, but as with trust itself, they are "built into the individual's personality" (420) as the basis for hope, meaning, faith, and all later pursuits. In essence, the individual's life of hope and meaning continually draws upon the mother's inner presence.

The idea of God as an abiding and protective inner presence is so pervasive in Western religious life that no particular references are probably required. Still, a single expression, once again from Rosenzweig's *Star*, should suffice: "The soul is tranquil in God's love, like a child in the arms of its mother, and now it can go to the farthest sea and to the gates of the grave—it always stays near Him" (2005, 185). The not unexpected gender rendering, of "Him" rather than possibly Her, in deference to patriarchy,[6] is all that mars the example from fitting perfectly with Winnicott's insight that "there is always someone present, someone who is equated ultimately and unconsciously with the mother" (1958, 420).[7]

As Chapter 4 relates, trust in God is a key feature of religious experience, which supports trust in the self (one's goodness, hope), other persons (their concern and reliability), and the world (its meaning and justice). These themes are expressed throughout the work of Buber, Heschel, and Levinas, and are briefly albeit eloquently expressed by Rosenzweig:

> To walk humbly with your God—nothing more is asked for here than a wholly present trust. But trust is a great word. It is the seed from which faith, hope and love grow, and the fruit that ripens from it.
>
> (2005, 447)

There is an important supplement to the idea of the individual carrying a supportive inner personal presence, whether of the mother or the divine. Bessel Van der Kolk details the meaning for victims of trauma, as well as in terms of overall psychological health, of feeling that others are aware and sympathetic, what he terms "being truly heard and seen by the people around us, feeling that we are held in someone else's mind and heart" (2015, 81). This being "held in someone else's mind and heart," the feeling that the individual is not just alone in an uncaring world, echoes Benjamin's view of the importance of being recognized by another. It also parallels an enduring legacy of the notion of God as person, in the idea that God holds each unique human creature in mind, which conveys the affective essence of the notions of revelation and providence. In his reading of the biblical love poem *Song of Songs*, the blueprint for revelation, Rosenzweig depicts God as the partner who initiates the love relationship and reaffirms its reality "in every moment" (2005, 175). Buber's understanding of providence is both personal and active: the "meaning we receive can be put to the proof in action only by each person in the uniqueness of his being and the uniqueness of his life" (1970, 159).

The notion of a personal God constitutes an indispensable aspect of the prominence of intersubjectivity in the work of the Jewish philosophers. The encounter with other persons and the encounter with the divine continually reinforce each other. This is a fundamental theme in Buber's *I and Thou*, as, in his words, "the close association of the relation to God with the relation to one's fellow-men … is my most essential concern" (1970, 171). His book portrays the relationship to others as the indispensable prerequisite for the relationship to God and insists that the I–Thou dialogue with God is an extension of those former relationships (123). Rosenzweig sees the biblical anthropomorphisms, which exemplify the idea of God as a person, as having the same supreme importance for Judaism as do "the Law and the Prophets" (1998, 143). Once again, his examination of the *Song of Songs* reveals the essence of the meeting with God. In its lines, the exchange of "I" and "Thou" between persons, through speech and love, both echoes and partakes of the human encounter with the divine. Rosenzweig writes, "The I and You of the inter-human language are also quite simply the I and You between God and man," and "Man loves because, and as, God loves" (2005, 214). Lastly, Levinas finds that through the "spiritual optics" of ethics a trace of the divine is evoked in the face of the other, writing,

> The dimension of the divine opens forth from the human face. ... The Other [the stranger, orphan, and widow] is not the incarnation of God, but precisely by his face, in which he is disincarnate, is the manifestation of the height in which God is revealed.
>
> (1969, 78–79)

A final note

Some interdisciplinary suggestions might be seen to issue from this investigation of *Trust and Trauma*. Academic programs in Philosophy would do well to include a significant component dedicated to recent breakthroughs in developmental psychology, focusing especially upon the mother-infant dyad. These findings have indisputable relevance to such perennial topics as subjectivity, mind, language, and emotions. Practitioners in the disciplines of Philosophy and Religious Studies might find important resources in post-Freudian developments in some streams of psychoanalysis, which feature innovative discussions about trust, meaning, and responsibility. Lastly, it is hoped that philosophers and psychologists might overcome their traditional suspicion, if not complete dismissal, of religious discourse as illusory and dysfunctional. As exemplified here, just as trust in God is analogous in many ways to basic trust, it is not worlds apart, or even a world apart, in its vulnerability or resilience to trauma.

Notes

1 James explains that the category of the "sick soul" refers to the perspective that "the evil aspects of our life are of its very essence" (2004, 98), and, on the other hand, his treatment of saintliness explores to what extent "the religious life commends itself as an ideal kind of human activity" (246).
2 This overview is revised from the presentation in the author's earlier book (Oppenheim 2017, 39–40).
3 Mitchell illustrates this dynamic between intrapsychic and interpersonal processes in terms of a Möbius strip "in which internal and external are perpetually regenerating and transforming themselves and each other" (2000, 57).
4 See the author's *Contemporary Psychoanalysis and Modern Jewish Philosophy* (Oppenheim 2017, 76–77).
5 Instead of regarding the isolated individual as the proper subject of Philosophy, which leads to the ongoing philosophic conundrum about the existence of other minds, Winnicott's understanding that being with others—intersubjectivity—is

the natural environment of human life, brings him to query about the possibility of being alone.

6 There is a discussion of feminist critiques of the Jewish philosophers, especially Luce Irigaray's examination of Levinas, in the author's *Jewish Philosophy and Psychoanalysis* (Oppenheim 2006, 175–219).

7 The role of the feminine *Shekinah* in Judaism and Mary in Christianity are just two examples of the religious provision of a close feminine presence.

References

Aron, Lewis. 1996. *A Meeting of Minds: Mutuality in Psychoanalysis*. Hillsdale, NJ: The Analytic Press.

———. 2016. "Mutual Vulnerability: An Ethic of Clinical Practice." In *The Ethical Turn: Otherness and Subjectivity in Contemporary Psychoanalysis*, edited by David M. Goodman and Eric R. Severson, 19–41. New York: Routledge.

Benjamin, Jessica. 1988. *The Bonds of Love: Psychoanalysis, Feminism, and the Problem of Domination*. New York: Pantheon Books.

———. 1995. *Like Subjects, Love Objects: Essays on Recognition and Sexual Difference*. New Haven, CT: Yale University Press.

———. 1998. *Shadow of the Other: Intersubjectivity and Gender in Psychoanalysis*. New York: Routledge.

———. 1999. "Recognition and Destruction: An Outline of Intersubjectivity." In *Relational Psychoanalysis: The Emergence of a Tradition*, edited by Stephen A. Mitchell and Lewis Aron, 181–210. Hillsdale, NJ: The Analytic Press.

———. 2004. "Beyond Doer and Done To: An Intersubjective View of Thirdness." *Psychoanalytic Quaterly* 73: 5–46.

———. 2007. "Intersubjectivity, Thirdness, and Mutual Recognition: A Talk Given at the Institute for Contemporary Psychoanalysis, Los Angeles, CA." *Institute for Contemporary Psychoanalysis*. http://icpla.edu/wp-content/uploads/2013/03/Benjamin-J.-2007-ICP-Presentation-Thirdness-present-send.pdf.

———. 2009. "Psychoanalytic Controversies: A Relational Psychoanalysis Perspective on the Necessity of Acknowledging Failure in order to Restore the Facilitating and Containing Features of the Intersubjective Relationship (the Shared Third)." *The International Journal of Psychoanalysis* 90: 441–450.

———. 2010. "Can We Recognize Each Other? Response to Donna Orange." *International Journal of Psychoanalytic Self Psychology* 5: 244–256.

———. 2012. "Beyond Doer and Done To: An Intersubjective View of Thirdness." In *Relational Psychoanalysis Vol. 4: Expansion of Theory*, edited by Lewis Aron and Adrienne Harris, 91–130. New York: Routledge.

———. 2014a. "The Discarded and the Dignified – Parts 1 and 2: From the Failed Witness to 'You Are the Eyes of the World.'" *Public Seminar*. www.publicseminar.org/2014/12/the-discarded-and-the-dignified-parts-1-and-2/.

———. 2014b. "The Discarded and the Dignified – Part 3: From the Failed Witness to 'You Are the Eyes of the World.'" *Public Seminar*. www.publicseminar.org/2014/12/the-discarded-and-the-dignified-part-3/.

———. 2014c. "The Discarded and the Dignified – Parts 4 and 5: From the Failed Witness to 'You Are the Eyes of the World.'" *Public Seminar*. www.publicseminar.org/2014/12/the-discarded-and-the-dignified-parts-4-and-5/.

———. 2014d. "The Discarded and the Dignified – Part 6: From the Failed Witness to 'You Are the Eyes of the World.'" *Public Seminar*. www.publicseminar.org/2014/12/the-discarded-and-the-dignified-part-6/.

———. 2016a. "Intersubjectivity." In *The Routledge Handbook of Psychoanalysis in the Social Sciences and Humanities*, edited by Anthony Elliott and Jeffrey Prager, 149–168. London: Routledge.

———. 2016b. "Non-Violence as Respect for All Suffering: Thoughts Inspired by Eyad el Sarraj." *Psychoanalysis, Culture and Society* 21: 5–20.

———. 2018. *Beyond Doer and Done To: Recognition Theory, Intersubjectivity and the Third*. New York: Routledge.

Berkovits, Eliezer. 1977. *Faith after the Holocaust*. New York: KTAV.

Berkson, William, and Menachem Fisch. 2010. *Pirke Avot: Timeless Wisdom for Modern Life*. Philadelphia: Jewish Publication Society.

Bonhoeffer, Dietrich. 1959. *Prisoner for God: Letters and Papers from Prison*. Edited by Eberhard Bethge. Translated by Reginald H. Fuller. New York: The Macmillan Company.

Bragin, Martha. 2007. "Knowing Terrible Things: Engaging Survivors of Extreme Violence in Treatment." *Clinical Social Work Journal* 35: 229–236.

Buber, Martin. 1952. *Eclipse of God: Studies in the Relation between Religion and Philosophy*. New York: Harper and Row.

———. 1965. *Between Man and Man*. New York: Macmillan Publishing Company.

———. 1967a. "Autobiographical Fragments." In *The Philosophy of Martin Buber*, edited by Paul Arthur Schilpp and Maurice Friedman, 3–39. La Salle, IL: Open Court.

———. 1967b. *On Judaism*. New York: Schocken Books.

———. 1967c. "Replies to My Critics." In *The Philosophy of Martin Buber*, edited by Paul Arthur Schilpp and Maurice Friedman, 689–744. La Salle, IL: Open Court.

———. 1970. *I and Thou*. Translated by Walter Kaufmann. New York: Charles Scriber's Sons.

———. 1999. *A Believing Humanism: My Testament, 1902–1965*. Translated by Maurice Friedman. Amherst, NY: Humanity Books.

———. 2003a. "A Response to a Letter from Ernsz Szilagyi, June 29, 1950." In "Agonism in Faith: Buber's Eternal Thou after the Holocaust," by David Forman-Barzilai. *Modern Judaism* 23 (2): 172–173.

———. 2003b. *Two Types of Faith*. Translated by Norman P. Goldhawk. Syracuse, NY: Syracuse University Press.

Buelens, Geret, Sam Durrant, and Robert Eaglestone. 2014. *The Future of Trauma Theory: Contemporary Literary and Cultural Criticism*. New York: Routledge.

Butler, Judith. 2006. *Precarious Life: The Powers of Mourning and Violence*. Brooklyn, NY: Verso Books.

Cesario, Joseph, David J. Johnson, and Heather L. Eisthen. 2020. "Your Brain is Not an Onion with a Tiny Reptile Inside." *Current Directions in Psychological Science* 29: 255–260.

Chester, Michael A. 2005. *Divine Pathos and Human Being: The Theology of Abraham Joshua Heschel*. Portland, OR: Vallentine Mitchell.

Coates, Susan W. 2005. "Having a Mind of One's Own and Holding the Other in Mind: Commentary on Paper by Peter Fonagy and Mary Target (1998)." In *Relational Psychoanalysis, Volume 2: Innovation and Expansion*, edited by Lewis Aron and Adrienne Harris, 279–310. Hillsdale, NJ: The Analytic Press.

Cohen, Arthur A. 1981. *The Tremendum: A Theological Interpretation of the Holocaust*. New York: Crossroad.

Eisen, Robert. 2003. "A. J. Heschel's Rabbinic Theology as a Response to the Holocaust." *Modern Judaism* 23 (3): 211–225.

Erikson, Erik H. 1963. *Childhood and Society*. New York: W.W. Norton and Co.

———. 1964. *Insight and Responsibility: Lectures on the Ethical Implications of Psychoanalytic Insight*. New York: W.W. Norton and Co.

———. 1968. *Identity: Youth and Crisis*. New York: W.W. Norton and Co.

———. 1969. *Gandhi's Truth: On the Origins of Militant Nonviolence*. New York: W.W. Norton and Co.

———. 1997. *The Life Cycle Completed: Extended Version with New Chapters on the Ninth Stage of Development by Joan M. Erikson*. New York: W.W. Norton and Co.

Even-Chen, Alexander, and Meir Ephraim. 2012. *Between Heschel and Buber: A Comparative Study*. Brighton, MA: Academic Studies Press.

Fackenheim, Emil L. 1968. *Quest for Past and Future: Essays in Jewish Theology*. Boston: Beacon Press.

———. 1978. *The Jewish Return into History: Reflections in the Age of Auschwitz and a New Jerusalem*. New York: Schocken Books.

———. 1982. *To Mend the World: Foundations of Future Jewish Thought*. New York: Schocken Books.

Faierstein, Morris M. 1999. "Abraham Joshua Heschel and the Holocaust." *Modern Judaism* 19 (3): 255–275.

Ferenczi, Sándor. 1988. *The Clinical Diary of Sándor Ferenczi*. Edited by Judith Dupont and translated by Michael Balint and Nicola Zarday Jackson. Cambridge, MA: Harvard University Press.

Forman-Barzilai, David. 2003. "Agonism in Faith: Buber's Eternal Thou after the Holocaust." *Modern Judaism* 23 (2): 156–179.

Freud, Sigmund. 1964. *The Future of an Illusion*. Translated by W.D. Robson-Scott. Revised and newly edited by James Strachey. Garden City, NY: Anchor Books, Doubleday and Company.

Friedman, Maurice, ed. 1973. *Meetings: Martin Buber*. La Salle, IL: Open Court.

———. 1988. *Martin Buber's Life and Work: The Middle Years, 1923–1945*. Detroit: Wayne State University Press.

Gana, Nouri. 2014. "Trauma Ties: Chiasmus and Community in Lebanese Civil War Literature." In *The Future of Trauma Theory: Contemporary Literary and Cultural Criticism*, edited by Gert Buelens, Samuel Durrant, and Robert Eaglestone, 77–90. London and New York: Routledge.

Gerson, Samuel. 2004. "The Relational Unconscious: A Core Element of Intersubjectivity, Thirdness, and Clinical Progress." *Psychoanalytic Quarterly* 73 (1): 63–98.

———. 2009. "When the Third Is Dead: Memory, Mourning, and Witnessing in the Aftermath of the Holocaust." *The International Journal of Psychoanalysis* 90: 1341–1357.

Glatzer, Nahum N., ed. 1955. *On Jewish Learning: Franz Rosenzweig*. New York: Schocken Books.

Goodman, David M. and Eric R. Severson, eds. 2016. *The Ethical Turn: Otherness and Subjectivity in Contemporary Psychoanalysis*. New York: Routledge.

Herman, Judith. 2015. *Trauma and Recovery: The Aftermath of Violence—From Domestic Abuse to Political Terror*. New York: Basic Books.

Heschel, Abraham Joshua. 1951. *Man is not Alone: A Philosophy of Religion.* New York: Harper and Row.

———. 1955. *God in Search of Man: A Philosophy of Judaism.* New York: Harper and Row.

———. 1969. *Israel: An Echo of Eternity.* New York: Farrar, Straus and Giroux.

———. 1972. *The Insecurity of Freedom: Essays on Human Existence.* New York: Schocken Books.

———. 1974. *A Passion for Truth.* New York: Farrar, Straus and Giroux.

———. 2007. *Heavenly Torah: As Refracted through the Generations.* New York: Bloomsbury.

———. 2009. "No Religion Is an Island." In *No Religion Is an Island: Abraham Joshua Heschel and Interreligious Dialogue*, edited by Harold Kasimow and Byron L. Sherman, 3–22. Eugene, OR: Wipf and Stock.

Heschel, Susannah. 2016. "Trauma, Jews, and Gender—How They Are Transmitted, Imagined, and Reconceived: Response to Judith Alpert and Jill Salberg." In *The Ethical Turn: Otherness and Subjectivity in Contemporary Psychoanalysis*, edited by David M. Goodman and Eric R. Severson, 178–185. New York: Routledge.

Irigaray, Luce. 1985. *Speculum of the Other Woman.* Translated by Gillian C. Gill. Ithaca, NY: Cornell University Press.

James, William. 2004. *The Varieties of Religious Experience: A Study of Human Nature.* New York: Simon and Schuster.

Kaplan, Edward K. 1996. *Holiness in Words: Abraham Joshua Heschel's Poetics of Piety.* Albany: State University of New York Press.

Kaplan, Edward K., and Samuel H. Dresner. 1998. *Abraham Joshua Heschel: Prophetic Witness.* New Haven: Yale University Press.

Katz, Steven T. 1980. "Abraham Joshua Heschel and Hasidism." *Journal of Jewish Studies* 31 (Spring): 82–104.

Kierkegaard, Søren. 1968. *Concluding Unscientific Postscript to the Philosophical Fragments* [by Johannes Climacus]. Translated by David F. Swenson and Walter Lowrie. Princeton, NJ: Princeton University Press.

———. 1980. *The Sickness unto Death: A Christian Psychological Exposition for Upbringing and Awakening* [by Anti-Climacus]. Edited and translated by Howard V. Hong and Edna H. Hong. Princeton, NJ: Princeton University Press.

———. 1995. *Works of Love.* Edited and translated by Howard V. Hong and Edna H. Hong. Princeton, NJ: Princeton University Press.

Kristeva, Julia. 1982. *Powers of Horror: An Essay on Abjection.* Translated by Leon S. Roudiez. New York: Columbia University Press.

Lawritson, Jerry D. 1996. "Martin Buber and the Shoah." In *Martin Buber and the Human Sciences*, edited by Maurice Friedman, 295–309. Albany: State University of New York Press.

Levinas, Emmanuel. 1969. *Totality and Infinity: An Essay on Exteriority.* Translated by Alphonso Lingis. Pittsburgh, PA: Duquesne University Press.

———. 1981. *Otherwise than Being or Beyond Essence.* Translated by Alphonso Lingis. The Hague, Netherlands: Martinus Nihoff.

———. 1985. *Ethics and Infinity: Conversations with Philippe Nemo.* Translated by Richard A. Cohen. Pittsburgh, PA: Duquesne University Press.

———. 1987. "Language and Proximity." In *Collected Philosophical Papers*, translated by Alphonso Lingis, 109–126. Pittsburg, PA: Duquesne University Press.

———. 1990. *Difficult Freedom: Essays on Judaism*. Translated by Seán Hand. Baltimore: Johns Hopkins University Press.

———. 1996. *Emmanuel Levinas: Basic Philosophical Writings*. Edited by Adriaan T. Peperzak, Simon Critchley, and Robert Bernasconi. Bloomington, IN: Indiana University Press.

———. 1998. *Entre Nous: On Thinking-of-the-Other*. Translated by Michael B. Smith and Barbara Harshav. New York: Columbia University Press.

———. 2001. *Is it Righteous to Be?: Interviews with Emmanuel Levinas*. Edited by Jill Robbins. Stanford: Stanford University Press.

Loewald, Hans W. 1978. *Psychoanalysis and the History of the Individual: The Freud Lectures at Yale*. New Haven, CT: Yale University Press.

———. 2000. *The Essential Loewald: Collected Papers and Monographs*. Hagerstown, MD: University Publishing Group.

McNally, Richard J. 2005. "Debunking Myths about Trauma and Memory." *The Canadian Journal of Psychiatry* 50: 817–822.

Mendes-Flohr, Paul R. 2019. *Martin Buber: A Life of Faith and Dissent*. New Haven and London: Yale University Press.

Mendes-Flohr, Paul R., ed. 1983. *A Land of Two Peoples: Martin Buber on Jews and Arabs*. New York: Oxford University Press.

———. 1988. *The Philosophy of Franz Rosenzweig*. Boston: Brandeis University Press.

Mitchell, Stephen A. 1993. *Hope and Dread in Psychoanalysis*. New York: Basic Books.

———. 2000. *Relationality: From Attachment to Intersubjectivity*. Hillsdale, NJ: The Analytic Press.

Morgan, Michael L., ed. 1987. *The Jewish Thought of Emil Fackenheim: A Reader*. Detroit: Wayne State University Press.

Oppenheim, Michael. 1997. *Speaking/Writing of God: Jewish Philosophical Reflections on the Life with Others*. Albany: State University of New York Press.

———. 2006. *Jewish Philosophy and Psychoanalysis: Narrating the Interhuman*. Lanham, MD: Lexington Books.

———. 2009. *Encounters of Consequence: Jewish Philosophy in the Twentieth Century and Beyond*. Brighton, MA: Academic Studies Press.

———. 2017. *Contemporary Psychoanalysis and Modern Jewish Philosophy: Two Languages of Love*. New York: Routledge.

Orange, Donna M. 2011. *The Suffering Stranger: Hermeneutics for Everyday Practice*. New York: Routledge.

———. 2016. *Nourishing the Inner Life of Clinicians and Humanitarians: The Ethical Turn in Psychoanalysis*. New York: Routledge.

Putnam, Hilary. 2008. *Jewish Philosophy as a Guide to Life: Rosenzweig, Buber, Levinas, Wittgenstein*. Bloomington, IN: Indiana University Press.

Rorty, Richard. 1987. "Pragmatism and Philosophy." In *After Philosophy: End or Transformation?*, edited by Kenneth Baynes, James Bohman, and Thomas McCarthy, 26–66. Cambridge, MA: MIT Press.

Rosenstock-Huessy, Eugen., ed. 1971. *Judaism Despite Christianity: The "Letters on Christianity and Judaism" between Eugen Rosenstock-Huessy and Franz Rosenzweig*. New York: Schocken Books.

Rosenzweig, Franz. 1998. *God, Man, and the World: Lectures and Essays*. Edited and translated by Barbara E. Galli. Syracuse, NY: Syracuse University Press.

———. 1999a. *Franz Rosenzweig's "The New Thinking."* Edited and translated by Alan Udoff and Barbara E. Galli. Syracuse, NY: Syracuse University Press.

———. 1999b. *Understanding the Sick and the Healthy: A View of World, Man, and God.* Edited and translated by Nahum Glatzer. Cambridge, MA: Harvard University Press.

———. 2005. *The Star of Redemption.* Translated by Barbara E. Galli. Madison, WI: University of Wisconsin Press.

Rubenstein, Richard L. 1966. *After Auschwitz: Radical Theology and Contemporary Judaism.* Indianapolis: Bobbs-Merrill.

Schlein, Stephen. 2016. *The Clinical Erik Erikson: A Psychoanalytic Method of Engagement and Activation.* New York: Routledge.

Sporns, Olaf. 2007. "Brain Connectivity." *Scholarpedia* 2 (10): 4695.

Stolorow, Robert D. 2007. *Trauma and Human Existence: Autobiographical, Psychoanalytic and Philosophical Reflections.* New York: The Analytic Press.

Tutu, Desmond Mpilo. 1999. *No Future without Forgiveness.* New York: Doubleday.

Van der Kolk, Bessel. 2015. *The Body Keeps the Score: Brain, Mind, and Body in the Healing of Trauma.* New York: Penguin Books.

Vermeulen, Pieter. 2014. "The Biopolitics of Trauma." In *The Future of Trauma Theory: Contemporary Literary and Cultural Criticism*, edited by Gert Buelens, Samuel Durrant, and Robert Eaglestone, 141–155. London and New York: Routledge.

Wiesel, Elie. 1979. "Why I Write." In *Confronting the Holocaust: The Impact of Elie Wiesel*, edited by Alvin H. Rosenfeld and Irving Greenberg, 200–206. Bloomington: Indiana University Press.

———. 1995. *All Rivers Run to the Sea: Memoirs.* Toronto: Alfred A. Knopf Canada.

———. 2000. "A Plea for the Dead." In *A Holocaust Reader: Responses to the Nazi Extermination*, edited by Michael L. Morgan, 67–77. New York: Oxford University Press.

Winnicott, D. W. 1958. "The Capacity to Be Alone." *International Journal of Psycho-Analysis* 39: 416–420.

Index

For Product Safety Concerns and Information please contact our EU
representative GPSR@taylorandfrancis.com
Taylor & Francis Verlag GmbH, Kaufingerstraße 24, 80331 München, Germany

9 780367 458706